Hampton-in-Arden

At the Millennium

Hampton-in-Arden

At the Millennium

Compiled and edited by
Mike Bryant, Ray Parker and Harry Smith

BREWIN
BOOKS

First published in 2000 by
Brewin Books, Studley, Warwickshire B80 7LG

British Library Cataloguing in Publication Data
A catalogue record for this book is available from
The British Library

ISBN: 1 85858 164 8

Typeset in Baskerville and made and printed
in Great Britain by Warwick Printing Company Limited,
Theatre Street, Warwick, Warwickshire CV34 4DR.

CONTENTS

ACKNOWLEDGEMENTS

The editors would like to thank the large number of people who helped make this book happen. Therefore the first thank you must be to all the contributors who produced the words and in a lot of cases the photographs as well. Thank you all very much indeed. In addition to these we then had to call on extra help to produce some more photographs, and we sincerely thank Pamela Parker and Michael Wells for their help.

But this was a group effort by the Local History Group plus two very willing volunteers, Ray Parker and Harry Smith. None of this would have happened without the support of John Barton, David Hill, Malcolm James, Robin Watkin and other members of the Local History Group. We are especially grateful to Robin for the drawing of the two maps as well as writing several sections. Then a special thank you to Beryl Bryant for typing all the words into something which we could then pass to the printers.

We must not forget the large number of other people who have given us encouragement in various ways during the gestation period of this book. Thank you all.

INTRODUCTION TO THE BOOK

As the millennium, approached a village co-ordination group was formed consisting of representatives from the Church, the Parish Council and the Hampton Society. At an early meeting a suggestion was made that a record be made of what life in Hampton-in-Arden was like at the turn of the millennium. Michael Child, of the Hampton Society, undertook to take the matter up with the Society; the Local History group agreed to take it on board as a project.

At one of its regular meetings the Group considered various methods of recording information on tapes, videos, and ROM discs and finally decided on a printed book containing descriptions and photographs of a cross-section of village social and working activities. And so the idea of the Hampton-in-Arden Millennium Book was born – and that was the easy part!

The first task was to produce a comprehensive list of all village activities, from businesses and shops to social clubs and organisations, and including services from inside and outside the village. The resulting list, when finally completed, added up to nearly fifty groups that made up the structure of the village. At this point we were confronted with the realization that we had embarked upon a daunting and seemingly impossible task.

In the following months many people in the village were asked to give time, effort and dedication to bring this work to a satisfactory conclusion. A letter explaining the project and requesting a four-hundred-word statement of their activity, and involvement in the life of the village (together with photographs) no doubt caused much apprehension (if not panic) for some who had not written a four-hundred-word essay since their school days. They rose to the occasion, however, and are to be congratulated for their efforts. Many submitted photographs of their activities and where, in certain cases, this was not possible, members of the village photographic club offered their services, for which we are extremely grateful.

The book is not written as a history of the village, nor does it conventionally have a single author: it is a snapshot of this time, compiled from a series of profiles submitted by members of the village, recording the working structure and social fabric of life in Hampton-in-Arden. It is intended for the enjoyment of villagers in the present and the interest, and possibly hilarity and astonishment of villagers in the future.

To all those people who found the time and made the effort to bring this project alive, this book is gratefully dedicated.

AN INTRODUCTION TO THE VILLAGE

Hampton-in-Arden is a small village (originally in Warwickshire but now in the Metropolitan Borough of Solihull). It is situated between Solihull and Coventry, close to the village of Meriden, alleged to be the geographic centre of England.

In the past this was a tiny hamlet formed by a few cottages around the church housing the farm labourers, who travelled each day to the open fields and then later on to the farms in the surrounding area.

The railway, built in 1838 across the northern border of the village, caused a great social change to life in the village. Much later a similar upheaval occurred when motorways were constructed in the area. The ease of commuting introduced a new type of inhabitant to the village: those requiring the peace of a rural retreat with the mobility by rail and road to the modern industrial and commercial centres of the midlands.

The area of the village is about 103 hectares (254 acres), set in a Parish area which is some five or six times larger. The population is between 1,800 and 1,900 of whom approximately 400 are under the age of 17. The village is a popular place in which to live which probably accounts for a relatively high number of residents over 60. A lot of the residents have moved house several times within the village as their housing needs have changed. But they like it here and so stay in the village.

The top of the village.

The village has a church, a junior and infants school with a fairly new nursery unit, a number of shops including a chemist, two public houses and a number of halls for general use. Sporting activities – cricket, tennis, hockey, football and bowls – have been prominent in the village for over a hundred years. Craft activities and social clubs are many and varied, and are well attended by all age groups.

Hampton is a village which is continually under threat from developers of one sort or another. The threat of development within the village itself or on the land around the village. At present there are three applications for permission to build Motorway Service Areas in the Solihull area. One of these is on land adjacent to Walford Hall Farm House, directly alongside Solihull Road opposite to Hampton Lane Farm. A Public Inquiry started on 30th November 1999 scheduled to finish on 11th February 2000. It met again in May and June 2000 and a decision is not expected until 2001.

In situations like this the village residents unite against the proposals. But like many other villages it can also become divided internally on various issues. The most recent of these was the proposal by the Sports Club for a floodlit astroturf pitch and a replacement clubhouse to include a leisure pool and gym all on the Village Recreation Ground. Following a Public Inquiry the Secretary of State for the Environment, Transport and the Regions has rejected the applications as being inappropriate in the Green Belt. The village now has to unite to achieve improved sporting and leisure facilities.

Hampton-in-Arden has seen many changes in its time, both physical and social, and there is no doubt that change will continue. With the increasing need for building land, the local Parish Council and the Hampton-in-Arden Society will be required to stand their ground to maintain the character of the village.

The bottom of the village.

Chapter One:

The Village Infrastructure

Hampton has a church, which is mentioned in the Domesday Book. This was probably a wooden structure, and the earliest part of the current church was built in about 1130 AD. The church occupies the highest site in the village, and adjacent to it is the original medieval manor house, now a private house called the Moat House; immediately across the road is the timber framed White Lion. The village still has a school; the original boys-only school merged much later with the Girls' and Infants' School as a result of the 1944 Education Act, and we now have a Junior and Infants School. Since 1944, after the age of eleven children now have to attend a school outside the village.

Local affairs are in the hands of the Hampton-in-Arden Parish Council. The village is fortunate in having a Charitable Foundation, which was originally devoted to the education of village boys, but which now has a much wider remit and sufficient funds to help in the village in a number of different ways. The Fentham Trust has been instrumental in the building of the surgery upon Trust land, thereby ensuring the provision of a medical practice in the village.

The church.

PARISH CHURCH OF ST MARY AND ST BARTHOLOMEW

A church has been at the centre of village life since Saxon times. The Parish church now serves a larger and greatly changed community. Worship is at the centre of the Church's life, with a variety of services on a Sunday attracting an average congregation of about 130. On Festivals and special occasions such as Harvest and Remembrance, attendances can be between two and three hundred.

Rev John de Wit and Alan Warren in the entrance porch.

Hampton continues to have a resident parish priest, who is part-time, and two lay readers. The Parochial Church Council is the Church's governing body, but much of the day-to-day work is done by the PCC's sub-committees. These committees concern themselves with mission and evangelism, Christian lay education and training, links with the wider church and the community, worship, maintenance of the Church, churchyard and church hall, and finance and Christian stewardship.

Mary and Tommy Weir are congratulated on their Golden Wedding.

The Church has a thriving Sunday Club for children and young people, and an active choir and a bell ringing team.

At the moment the PCC is consulting the community and the Diocese in the hope of launching a millennium building project. This will enlarge the vestry and provide additional facilities and meeting spaces within the church building, to assist with educational work and to offer more modern standards of hospitality to all who enter this ancient and beautiful building.

Inside the church at a parade/family service.

CHURCH CHOIR

Choirs have been helping to lead the worship in the church in Hampton for hundreds of years. Extant are the names of some twenty of the organists/choir masters who trained Hampton choirs. Latterly Dr Andrew Dicks was organist when the incumbent was the Rev Jack Adams, followed by Les Smith with Canon Harold Sly; Stuart Reeve and then David Dewar were organists when the Rev Alan Reynolds was the priest.

The choir processes down the church.

When the Rev Alan Reynolds left Hampton in 1994 to take up a ministry in Moseley, there was an interregnum, which lasted some 18 months, for David Dewar also left, and the village was without both minister and organist. Deputy organists had to be employed to play for Sunday services and choir practice, and would-be choristers were asked to swell the ranks (numbering about eight at the time). Surprisingly during this difficult period new people did join the choir and numbers rose to eighteen. Advertisements in the local press for a choir-master/organist produced a miracle and the Ashfields came.

In 1995 with the choir rebuilding, there still seemed to be a demand for traditional church music, which the Ashfield family felt called upon to encourage. After six months John de Wit was appointed as priest-in-charge and he skilfully sought to unite the different strands of church tradition at Hampton. Joint festival services with Bickenhill choir continued at Christmas and Easter. Besides supporting the church faithfully for 10:30 Communion or Family Service and 6:30pm Evensong, weddings and funerals, the choir has continued to develop

The choir is conducted by Christine Ashfield. Left rear stall front to back – Philippa Willetts, Alan Smyth and Tony Worthington. Left front stall – Haeni Kim, Bernice Griffiths and Nick Barnett. Right front stall – Susan Charlton, Heather Ashfield, Elizabeth Charlton, Charlotte Finch, Jean Hill and Michele Morton. Right rear stalls – Vickey Cardwell, Ursula Smyth, Betty Rackham, Felicity Biddle, Mollie Else, John Trumper and Michael Gough.

socially as well: attending annual RSCM festival services at Tewkesbury, Warwick and Birmingham; hosting the Organists' Association prestigious annual Evensong in 1997; and participating in annual outings to Manchester, Bath, Cambridge, York and Milford-on-Sea – some of which involved singing services away from home. All this has proved to be good experience and great fun.

Nick Barnett leads the choir and the procession to the War Memorial on Remembrance Sunday.

THE BELLRINGERS

The Bellringers, or the Society of Change Ringers as they should more properly be called, are an integral part of the church. Bells have been rung at Hampton-in-Arden since as long ago as 1524, when there were three bells in the tower. These bells probably perished in 1643 when the spire was struck by lightning.

A ring of six bells was cast by Joseph Smith of Edgbaston and installed in the tower in 1725. The present ring of eight bells superseded these in 1976, having been purchased from the redundant Church of St John, Miles Platting, Manchester.

Bell ringing – Ringing Master Brian Ellender and Alan Warren.

The present Society was formed in the early seventies with the object of raising funds to renovate and/or augment the six bells at the 250th anniversary of their casting in 1975, and also to advance the practice of change ringing in general.

Bells are the loud voice of the Church, speaking out over the community and calling the people to worship on Sundays, Church festivals and special occasions.

The particular pattern of swirling sounds made by our bells is to be found in England and in just a few other English-speaking countries. It is called change ringing where bells follow in certain sequences to form complex patterns of sound known as methods. Each bell changes one place every time it strikes and by regular practice the ringer can keep the standard as high as possible.

The bellringers are local people who have been head-hunted into joining the local band. They're normally, but not necessarily, members of the congregation. They are not paid, except for weddings. The main purpose is to ring before Sunday services. All ringers must be prepared and able to spend about one hour on most Sunday mornings. For training a weekly practice is essential.

Hampton-in-Arden has maintained a regular band of ringers for many years, but this has meant the constant training of new recruits. Short courses have been run through the Hampton Community Crafts, but individual tuition can always be arranged for anyone interested in pursuing this ancient art. Ringers do not have to be musical or good at maths, but just well-co-ordinated and have a sense of rhythm. Practice takes place on Monday evenings.

To celebrate the New Millennium thousands of recruits were trained to enable every church bell in the country to be rung at noon to *Ring in 2000*. Hampton trained two ringers for this purpose, which enabled all eight bells to be rung. The custom of ringing *the Old Year Out and the New Year In* was also resurrected after a lapse of some years. A certificate produced by the Central Council of Church Bellringers was presented to each ringer who took part on 1 January 2000. Long may this ancient art continue.

Bell ringing – left to right – Sue Restall, Roger Chapman, Cedric Goy, Philip Russell and Tim Iles.

SUNDAY CLUB

All the children and young people at Hampton Church belong to Sunday Club. They enjoy spending time with each other when they come together to make things, sing, listen to stories, cook and act. The activities are incorporated into a structured programme of Christian learning. The young people have their own special groups, which meet once a month. Over sixty children participate in the activities during the Parish Communion Service at 10:30am on Sundays.

The families all come together for a picnic in a village garden in the summer. Regular planning meetings for all the parents who are involved enable a varied programme of activities to be offered to all the children and young people. This year's programme has included outings to theatres, to see *Jesus Christ Super Star*, and a day trip in the summer term to visit the Black Country Museum, including a trip down a mine.

The Sunday Club.

THE CHURCH EMBROIDERY SCHEME

Early in 1998 the Church Links Committee, which fosters the encouragement of community projects within the village, proposed to make a needlework covering for the 'back to the wall' seating on the north and south sides of the church.

The north side was to be tackled first, and a faculty was obtained for permission to carry out this work. By generous donations from residents and Birmingham International Airport's Community Trust Fund, and proceeds from a big plant sale, sufficient funds were quickly raised.

Fortuitously the Reverend John de Wit, is also a Christian artist and he agreed to create twelve designs, inspired by artefacts in the church. In the months following, Nickie Blake studied the best way to carry out the scheme, reading up, visiting other churches, her own college – the Royal School of Needlework – embroidery shops and any other outlets which she thought might help.

Finally, on January 29 1999 the Links Committee and twelve enthusiastic village needlewomen met in the Church Hall. The designs, now traced onto canvas by Robin Watkin, were mounted on to twelve large individual frames made by John Cordwell, and the work was shared out among the group.

The Tent stitch used is worked diagonally across the canvas, which forms a firm woven effect on the wrong side – double thickness for the many years, which it is hoped the work will last. The team of embroiderers needed practice with this and the difficulties of stitching curves on canvas, but have met every month since to help each other along.

The first of the four cushions, which each contain three designs, is now being invisibly joined; progress is being made.

The Church Embroidery Scheme – from left Bessie Earnshaw, Margaret Mallin, Jean Amphlett, Janet Hardcastle, Jean Shepherd, Marjorie Iles, Rev John de Wit and Nickie Blake.

CHRISTIAN FOCUS

This is an ecumenical group for all ladies in the village, and meets on the first Monday of the month at 2pm in the Church Hall. There are about 40 members with a committee of eight; meetings are generally well attended.

Meetings are designed for members to enjoy a time of shared worship and prayer, to learn more about the worldwide church, to hear about and contribute to Christian charities and working groups, to inform each other of local Church activities and just to socialize.

During 1999 there was a demonstration of *Expressive Movement in Worship* and also a discussion about *Music in Worship*. Three Christian ladies talked autobiographically: one as an ordained minister; one as personal secretary to three bishops; and one as a dedicated teacher of deaf children. At other meetings the group learned about the Siloam ministry to children in Portugal and the Solihull Council of Churches Action for Homelessness. One occasion was devoted to a fascinating history of Hampton Church and its architecture, with an insight into the proposed alterations.

Every January members enjoy a *bring and share lunch*, which never fails to produce a delicious feast and fellowship to start the New Year. Other annual events are the summer outing, including a visit to a church – in 1999 to Leominster – and supporting the Women's World Day of Prayer and the Quiet Morning.

The meeting in December is always open to non-members and invited guests and concerns Advent. In 1999 Focus involved two friends with special skills in drama plus three men for the male parts to produce a thought-provoking, some-times humorous selection of sketches, litanies, music, participation and finally intercession for everyone's hopes for the coming year.

Christian Focus – from left: Mary Weir, Joan Lyons, Phil Dawson, Mary Barnett, Elsie Wright, Doraine Wilkinson, Hilary Crosby, Anne Grace, Mary Owen, Val Leitch, Dorothy Redgrave, Ann Keatley, Hilda Crowthers and Flix Haynes.

THE CHURCH AND VILLAGE CHRONICLE

The Chronicle aims to serve the church and village of Hampton-in-Arden by providing news each month about the activities of the church and a range of village organisations.

Each edition of the Chronicle reflects the range of activities, which occurs in Hampton. Regular contributions are received, for example, from Christian Focus, the Gardening Club, the Women's Institute, Probus, the Hockey Club, the Hampton Society and Hampton Community Crafts. An article by the vicar, John de Wit, a comprehensive village diary compiled by Flix Haynes and a record of baptisms, marriages and deaths in the parish are published each month. There is a well-established children's page and encouragement to care for and take interest in the natural beauty of our environment in *Conservation Conversation*.

The Chronicle is also a means of publicising the various events taking place in the village, or which are of interest to those in the locality. For example, the editions for December 1999 and January 2000 included details of village carol singing, a report on successful fund-raising for Macmillan Cancer Relief, events organised and planned by George Fentham School PTA, Millennium celebrations, a WI supper dance, a concert by the Hampton Singers, a *Theatrical Extravaganza* performed by the Hampton Players and the tenth anniversary celebrations of Age Concern Wednesday Club. They recorded fund-raising efforts by the Sunday Club and the Scouts and Guides Supporters' Association.

The Chronicle also reports general village news, striving to remain impartial in the face of any controversy. Reports are received from the Parish Council and in recent months the Chronicle has referred to plans for the motorway service area. The local doctor uses the magazine to update villagers on any changes or new equipment at the surgery, and the local library publicises its work through the Chronicle.

In recent years the Chronicle has received welcome funding from the Fentham Trust. The price for subscribers is also kept down by the support received from advertisers. They provide useful information for villagers on local firms, shops and services, as well as much-appreciated financial assistance.

Of course the Chronicle is what the church, villagers and village organisations make it. Over twenty volunteers are involved each month in compiling, editing and distributing the magazine. Its success and interest are totally dependent upon the range of interesting contributions which are submitted for publication each month and the willingness of members of the local community to buy the magazine.

THE GEORGE FENTHAM ENDOWED SCHOOL

The school has recently added an ICT (Information and Communication Technology) room, and the children were kept busy guessing what it would be like. The plan was to stock it with sixteen computers. The main school building

Key Stage 1 Assembly at the George Fentham Endowed School.

houses seven classrooms; a hall which is used for Assembly, PE and dinners; a PE store room; and a Resources room containing materials for Science, Technology and some Maths equipment. In a room in the Infant corridor groups of children do cooking, usually helped by volunteer parents. Upstairs is the Library. The Nursery unit is a separate building which has a main room, an activity room, a quiet room and its own playground. Mrs Algate is the teacher in charge and there is also a Nursery Nurse.

Children are taught three core curriculum subjects – Literacy, Maths and Science. The foundation subjects are Geography, History, Music, Technology, ICT, PE, Art and Religious Education.

Assembly at the George Fentham Endowed School, drawing by Joe Forrester aged 10.

Typical comments (from Class 6 aged 10/11) have included:

Excellent English: "Everyone might think it is about boring writing but our class makes it a totally different experience. For example, we tell each other our different opinions and hold debates. We act out stories and have interviews. We are learning things every day and it is fun."

Magnificent Maths: "In Numeracy lessons we learn lots of different things. To keep our maths brains bulging and alert we play maths games."

Playtime at the Nursery Unit.

Superb Silent Reading: "Silent reading is when we read in our head. It is a great way to calm down after the bustle of dinnertime."

Perfect PE: "We have lots of facilities in PE like crash mats, equipment for sports, a spring board and box, an elephant stand and, last but not least, two giant pieces of apparatus attached to the wall. We think it's great fun. We play netball, football and kwik cricket. In the summer term we do Athletics awards, *Ten Step* for Years 2-4 and *Five Star* for Years 5 and 6."

The children are divided into house teams of Blythe (blue), Aylesford (red), Arden (green) and Peel (yellow). Sports Day is held in July. Each child takes part in a class sprint and novelty race: Class 6 always seems to involve water! The afternoon ends with a House Relay race and a cup is awarded to the winning team. The boy and girl with the most points each win a special cup. (*Victor* and *Victrix Ludorum*)

After School clubs include Football, Rugby, Athletics, and Netball. On the music side there is Junior and Infant choir, keyboards and guitars. Peripatetic teaching staff are responsible for brass and woodwind instruction.

All classes make educational visits during the year. These range from local visits around the village, day visits in and around the West Midlands, and visits by Class 5 to Maengwynedd in Wales for three days and Class 6 to York for a week.

In the last few years there have been several new initiatives, which include an annual visit from Dave Shaw, *The Rainforest Man* who supported Class 5 in their study of the Amazon Rainforest. He brought in creatures such as millipedes, giant moths, tarantulas and stick insects. He also let children taste rainforest foods. They enjoyed mangoes, passion fruit, bananas, kiwi fruit and other exotic delights; and he painted faces with special tribal designs. Also included was an annual visit from Ian Blick *The Music Man* who worked with each class in turn. Mr Blick played the piano and members of the class played a variety of instruments from different parts of the world. At the end of the afternoon everyone played music together – always a big hit.

Mrs Taylor from Heart of England School's art department worked with Class 6. They made a clay gargoyle and then did some batik work. The children found it very exciting and Mrs Taylor was very pleased with the outcome.

The school uniform consists of grey trousers or skirts, grey or white shirts and maroon sweatshirts bearing the school logo. For PE children wear T-shirts, black shorts/games skirts and pumps indoors; trainers outdoors.

During playtimes children have the choice of two playgrounds: the bottom one for running and basketball, the top one for quieter activities.

The religious assembly is taken twice a week by Mr Wilkins, the Head teacher, and in turn by teachers on the other three days.

The positive atmosphere at the school seems to be appreciated by the children, who enjoy the learning process. Exciting times lie ahead.

The Nursery Unit, Mrs Algate teaches the children.

THE PARISH COUNCIL

Parishes date from medieval times, and in the 16th, 17th and 18th centuries they were the main unit of local government, responsible for poor relief, highway maintenance and law and order, as well as for their ecclesiastical functions. In the 19th century these civil functions were largely transferred to or taken over by other bodies. They have operated in their current form only since 1894. As a tier of local government they are elected bodies with discretionary powers and rights laid down by Parliament to represent their communities and to provide services for them.

The parish of Hampton-in-Arden is formed around a community of some 750 dwellings, with approximately 2000 residents. The Parish Council is an elected body of seven people, chosen to represent the views of the electors within the community ranging from local issues to major planning applications. Elections take place every four years.

The Parish Council has certain statutory powers, most of which are shared with the District Council of Solihull. It has no statutory duties to provide services, but its powers do permit it to offer facilities and to contribute towards the provision of facilities by others. They are principally of an environmental and recreational nature. A short list would include allotments, footpaths, playing fields, litter control, grass cutting etc. A good example is the recent installation of a children's playground built on ground adjacent to the allotments and near to the George Fentham School. Items installed include swings, slides and climbing apparatus.

The Parish Council Playground.

During the course of a year the full council holds regular meetings, with time set aside at each meeting for public participation. An annual meeting is also held, the purpose of which is to enable the Parish Council to report on its work over the past year to the residents. This is usually held in the Fentham Hall, which can accommodate some 200 people.

The Chairman of the Parish Council recently attended a public inquiry concerning a proposal to build a motorway service area alongside the M42 within the boundaries of the parish. This could have a tremendous impact on the village, both on the community and the environment surrounding it, if it were allowed to go ahead. It is the Parish Council's duty to respond to local issues like this on behalf of the community.

The Parish Council members at the year 2000 are Councillors Roger K Chapman (chairman), Julie A M Chavasse, Malcolm J James, Graham J Juniper, Bryonie A Kelly, Nigel R A Pettman and Alun L Thomas (vice-chairman).

THE PARISH COUNCIL ALLOTMENTS

The Parish Council has allotments in Fentham Road in part of the school playing fields. They are leased and controlled by the Council from the Fentham Trust and allotment holders pay a modest rent to the Council.

The Parish Council Allotments – Geoff Biggerstaff clearing the ground.

When the school nursery unit was opened several allotments were taken by the necessary car park. There are now five full-size plots, although most people find a half plot provides enough work and produce.

In 1999 there were eight allotment holders, the last plot being let in the autumn.

The soil is good and most people produce fine crops of vegetables.

THE GEORGE FENTHAM TRUST

Ten years after the Pilgrim Fathers set sail for America in 1620, a child was born in Hampton-in-Arden whose influence is still today an important feature in the fabric of community life.

George Fentham, the fifth child of Henry, grew up to be a successful business-man with interests centred on the developing city of Birmingham. Such evidence as we have points to the belief that George developed a keen sense of social responsibility and a clear awareness of the very real poverty then existing around him.

His last Will and Testament in 1690 reveals how he took the opportunity to make a lasting impact on shortcomings of his day. It stipulated how and where his estate was to be distributed, and particularly mentioned how he wished certain categories of persons *in the place of my nativity* (the manor of Hampton-in-Arden) to benefit from his personal estate.

At a time when unemployment was running at twenty per cent in the parish it was his special wish that his money should relieve and comfort the honest, deserving and industrious poor – but not *the idle and vitious*. In similar vein he left money for the provision of regular schooling in the village – formerly a somewhat hit-and-miss affair – and to this day these two objectives of deserving aid and education have been at the forefront of expenditure by the Trustees of the Charity.

By careful management over many generations his legacy has multiplied to levels, which have enabled many worthwhile projects to be completed within the area of benefit, and which happily perpetuate the name of George Fentham, benefactor to the village of Hampton-in-Arden.

The Fentham Trust and the Educational Foundation is made up of ten Trustees elected from the village: two by the SMBC; three by the Hampton-in-Arden Parish Council; one by the magistrates; and four co-opted by those so elected. Trustees serve a term of either three or four years from varying dates, thus ensuring continuity of direction. Trustees retiring are eligible for re-election. In addition a representative of Balsall Parish Council is invited to attend one meeting of the Educational Foundation each year.

The Fentham Trust's and Educational Foundation's principal activities at their quarterly meetings are to manage the properties and investments owned by the Trusts and ensure they are adequately maintained. A qualified firm of Surveyors and a national firm of Stockbrokers ably assist them.

The Trust properties include many acres of farmland, shops in Shirley, the Village Hall, Fentham Club, Doctor's Surgery, Crocketts Yard (three old cottages) and fifteen old people's bungalows on Fentham Green.

The Educational Foundation owns the School, the Nursery Unit and the playing fields and allotments to the side and rear.

Considerable funds are invested in blue chip securities to further the endowments for the area of benefit, which is the parish of Hampton-in-Arden as constituted on 23rd December 1907.

Seventeen persons who have lived in the village for at least two years occupy the Fentham Bungalows. The Trust gives weekly pensions to forty persons living in the village. Each year two students are given grants for a three-year period. Many grants are also given to encourage and help organisations in the village such as Scouts, Hampton Community Crafts, Playgroup, Players, Age Concern, Health, Sport and Education.

The Educational Foundation supports the School and Nursery Unit. It also annually gives grants to local schools in its area of benefit to enable them to buy books.

Recently the Fentham Trust agreed to make a considerable grant towards providing the village with a swimming pool and fitness centre, but this was considered to be an inappropriate development by a government appointed inspector.

George Fentham was a man with a vision and no doubt he would have been proud of the way the Trust has developed and flourished. Today's Trustees are determined to follow his example and plan improved facilities for all residents of the area of benefit in this 21st century, within the terms of the Trust.

HAMPTON MANOR

Over the last 150 years since Hampton Manor was built, it has evolved from being the family home of Sir Frederick Peel, son of the Prime Minister of 1841,

The Manor House from the lawns.

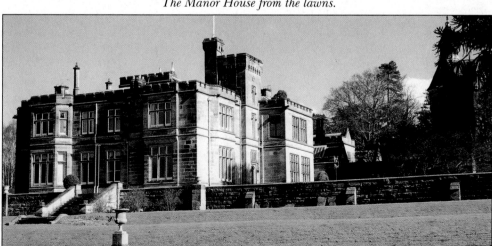

The Craft Hall at the Manor.

to the home of the Rollason family until 1952. It was then purchased by Mr and Mrs A J Jacobs as a home for 32 ladies disabled in some way and in need of support and care. Since the Community Care Act in 1984 people with disabilities have been given the same rights as those who are deemed to be normal and there are now far more opportunities for disabled people of all ages to have real choices and to live an independent and fulfilling life.

The way of life at Hampton Manor has changed to encompass this and the staff are constantly striving for the community to be aware that the people they care for have the right to be fully part of their community and have much to offer.

Hampton Manor is a privately owned and managed concern, though operating under the auspices of the Local Authority. It retains the ability to operate as an independent body in exercising all the best practices required by the Local Authority, but carrying out its own programmes of development and changes to suit the best perceived interests of the people in its care.

A Manor Craft Room.

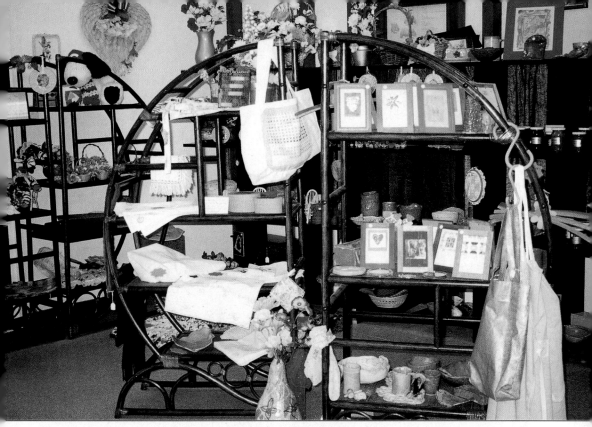

A display in the Craft Shop.

The ladies at the Manor enjoy mostly private sleeping accommodation, though preferences for sharing rooms is accommodated when possible. Rooms are very comfortable, tastefully decorated and contain furniture and fittings where possible of the residents' own choice. A communal dining room and several relaxation lounges are provided with quiet or shared activity areas available for use as required.

Many of the ladies, whatever their physical disabilities, do have their own special skills. These are expressed and developed in a special craft hall where such skills can be practised under professional guidance and the results offered for sale in their own craft shop.

Manor Allotments – Mary and Nick Barnett at work.

The ladies are further encouraged and helped to seek alternative activity off the Manor premises. For example, they enrol for courses at the local College of Further Education. They join in some village group activities such as Keep Fit and Flower Arranging, and attend church. Some have modest part-time jobs in the village.

The ladies of Hampton Manor have a full, varied and interesting life, with all the highs and lows experienced in any family. They have good reason to look forward to the start of the next millennium.

The extensive lawns, trees, greenhouses and grounds which surround the Manor are carefully attended by the gardeners and groundsmen.

The Manor walled-garden is used for allotments. In recent years the ladies of the Manor have looked after some of the plots, whilst other plots are let to members of the public. The area of the allotments is carefully attended by the Manor ground staff.

Approach to the Manor House at night.

THE COPTIC ORTHODOX CHURCH

In 1984 the Coptic Orthodox Church purchased the old Congregational Chapel which had not been used as such for a number of years. It was opened as the Coptic Orthodox Church of St. Mary and St. Anthony in 1985. Coptic means Egyptian and hence it is the Orthodox Church of Egypt. The Hampton church serves an area based on Birmingham with a radius of about 50 miles. Virtually the whole of the male congregation are doctors of one sort or another and they come from all around, from Northampton to Shrewsbury, from Derby to Redditch. None of the congregation lives in Hampton.

Chapter Two:

Village Organisations and Clubs

T here are a number of organisations within the village aimed at improving the quality of life of residents. Community Crafts runs courses on a wide variety of topics, and the Players put on a range of performances – of which the most popular are the comedies. The Singers cover a wide range of musical compositions which are always well supported. The Hampton Society is for those concerned with retaining the character of the village. Supporting the school in two different ways are the Parent Teachers Association and the Pre-school group who aim to catch them young.

The village has a wide range of clubs to enable residents to participate in many activities. We give below just some of the clubs which are listed in the village directory, plus some others which have come to our attention. But we know that a lot more activities take place behind closed doors and are just groups of residents that have a common interest. For example there are numerous bridge groups which have started from different sources but have in common a love of the game played amongst friends. There is also an investment club which originated in a village organisation but is really a group of friends pursuing a common interest.

AGE CONCERN WEDNESDAY CLUB

At ten o'clock most Wednesdays you may see the *helpers* arrive at the Arden Room to prepare for the Day Club. There are six helpers. At 10:30 am the Age Concern bus arrives with about 14 members, while others walk from their homes in Hampton. All members pay £3 to include coffee, lunch and tea, plus transport, entertainment and outings.

There is never a dull moment, as members exchange news, discuss world events, play Scrabble or card games, and eat and drink! There is a weekly *all bring, all win* raffle, which supplies funds for lunches at suitable hotels or pubs, which provides members with a ride into the countryside.

During term time the lunch is provided by the school but during school holidays the *helpers* have to use their cooking skills or occasionally resort to fish and chips!

Age Concern Solihull not only lays on the bus and attentive driver, but gives a lot of support with up-to-date information for OAPs and suggestions for

Age Concern Wednesday Club have a Christmas party.

speakers about relevant subjects. These have included CAB, Insurance, Making a Will, and Incontinence: the latter caused as much entertainment as it did information.

Music is in great demand and *Singing for Pleasure* and *U3A* groups are often asked to come and sing. On these occasions another Age Concern group is invited to boost the audience. This involves making tea and cakes for about 60 people! Another popular visitor is Diana Faultless LRAM (pianist), who plays classical music, which she introduces with biographical notes of the composers.

At Christmas the group decorates the room and holds an *Open Morning* for anyone in the village to join them for light refreshments and seasonal greetings. For the tenth anniversary in 1999 a beautiful cake was made and iced by two villagers. The Wednesday Club is adept at celebration, marking all festivals with a special lunch, table decorations and presents. In 1999 a mini harvest thanksgiving was held.

Many good friendships are made at this club. The chat and laughter are a great palliative, whatever the ailments. The Arden Room provides wonderful views of seasonal changes, and the members of the club are grateful to the Fentham Trust for covering the hire of the room.

Helpers at the Christmas Party, from left June Carter, Joan Lyons, Ivan Manders, Gloria Seabridge, Michael Wells, Audrey Wells and Margaret Fulford.

THE CAMERA CIRCLE

Three years ago Hampton Community Crafts asked Michael Wells to run a basic short course in photography. It was called *You and Your Camera* in the spring of 1996. Following that course students wanted photographic outings, such as the one which was called *Birmingham Cityscape,* and informal meetings. From that moment Hampton Camera Circle was born.

Camera Circle – Michael Wells and John Shalley take photographs from the top of the church tower.

The Circle is a small group of 16 members who own a variety of SLRs (single lens reflex), Compacts and APS (advanced photo system) cameras. The *Advanced Photo System* gives three different formats and a lot of scope for good pictures. It meets in alternate months to talk cameras, look at members' photos, view slides and hear visiting speakers. A great friend of the circle, Mike Albutt of Knowle Camera Club, ran workshops on the mounting and presentation of prints. Individual presentations have noticeably improved as a result.

A bi-monthly newsletter helps members to keep in touch. Meetings take place in the Fentham Trustees' room, upstairs in the Fentham Club. Continuing main activities include the Circle's display at the October Arts and Crafts Exhibition, both in the foyer and in the Arden Room, and the December Community Crafts display. The wide range of subjects and interpretations of the Circle's presentations have excited wide interest.

Notable photo outings were to the Butterfly Farm and Insect House at Stratford. The special tour conducted by the farm manager was a photographic feast. Next was a visit to Hampton Church tower: Brian Ellender, the ringing master, was the host, and all made the final climb to the parapet on the roof. Besides learning about the history of the bells the group enjoyed some photo opportunities.

Recently some members went to the Robert Capa Exhibition at Warwick Arts Centre. He was an outstanding photographer during the Spanish Civil War, noted for his stark action shots.

Each summer the Circle holds an informal meeting at a member's house. Last year the venue was Barbara Haddon's home. She is a *media* student at Birmingham University who has researched the history of photo albums from Victorian times. Members contributed with their own favourite albums, and wine and refreshments rounded off a very enjoyable evening.

Michael Wells and Peter Daniel and a Camera Circle display.

EXTEND

Extend – Movement to Music for men and women over 60 and disabled people of all ages – a registered charity, was founded in 1976. Its aims are to provide recreational exercise to music, stimulate health of body and mind, increase mobility and enhance the quality of life. Fully qualified teachers take classes throughout the UK in community, nursing and residential homes, sheltered housing and *special needs* clubs.

The Hampton Extenders' class started in September 1988, with nine members, in the Church Hall. Now membership exceeds 35, and meetings take place every Thursday morning in the Fentham Hall for an hour's exercise followed by coffee and chat. The Fentham Trust helps with the rent, for which the group is grateful.

Extending are – front row from left Maude Craig, Hilda Crothers and Dorothy Redgrave,
second row from left are Ann Keatley, Eve Baker and Joan Owen.

Extending in the Fentham Hall, front row from left Molly Else, Joan Lyons, Phil Dawson and Moira Kyles, second row from left Margaret Possart, Jean Cubbage, Mary Downing and Joan Owen.

Chair exercises and walking at each individual's pace are encouraged, despite varying disabilities (aches and pains); all are encouraged to participate. Apparatus such as scarves, balls, hoops and batons add further interest to the work. Routines are put together during the weeks to create *sequences*, so providing a sense of achievement.

Any excuse for a party! All major birthdays and anniversaries are marked by wine and good things to eat! Extend is proud to have two 90-year-old members (Maude Craig and Hilda Crothers) – both founder members, and also five octogenarians. Everyone benefits from their enthusiasm and also from that of the four girls from the Manor Home and their carer Wendy Stokes. There is so much interest in Extend's activities that the Hampton group has been asked to give demonstrations to various clubs, including Claverdon, Lapworth, and Manor Homes, to the WI in Hampton, Meriden, Shrewley and Marston Green.

Attending rallies is a popular feature, and Extenders countrywide meet for one big social event, usually in Luton or Burton-on-Trent. These trips involve a

Ladies from the Manor extending are, from left, Jane Jennens, Celia Longfield, Susan Pearson, Wendy Stokes, Pauline Vernon and Linda Payne.

happy minibus ride and more excuses for food and drink! About twice a year Hamptonians meet in the White Lion for a sandwich lunch, and laughter levels increase as the wine flows!

To raise funds for the organisation there are coffee mornings, a tea dance, Christmas decorations sale and Open Days.

Extend classes have become an important feature of the week for many, and provide fun, laughter and a place for friends to meet and catch up on village news, its people and events.

THE FENTHAM CLUB

The Fentham Club, originally known as the Fentham Institute, was established early in the 20th century and occupies the large white Georgian building adjacent to the Fentham Hall, the entrance being opposite Back Lane (Fentham Road). It is a private members' club, but offers its facilities for the use of villagers. Membership of the Club is open to all residents of the village, as well as people from the surrounding district. The property is owned by the George Fentham Trust and the Club leases the property from the Trust.

The Club has a long-established policy of providing for the social needs of the inhabitants of the village. In its origins this included use as the village Bath House. With the changes in housing amenities which have occurred since the 1920s this need has long since disappeared, and the Club has responded to change by aiming to provide a venue for all members of the family to enjoy themselves. Family Membership enables every one in the family to be involved in the Club. It is no longer an exclusive male preserve. The Club has a long-established relationship with Sheldon and District Charity, and has helped in raising funds for the Birmingham Children's Hospital and Children's Hospices.

The Fentham Club.

The premises include extensive grounds at the rear of the building, which are maintained by the Club. These grounds include a bowling green (which is open to play from the late spring till the autumn) as well as a children's play area.

The most spectacular view from the Club is that from the lounge, over the fields towards Barston and the lakes which have been created alongside the river Blythe. This is probably the ideal view of these scenic aspects of the village.

Within the Club a variety of games is played. The Club fields darts and domino teams who play in local leagues, maintaining contacts with other communities from the Warwickshire area. The Club also runs a variety of tournaments for members, including a doubles tournament in the spring and a singles tournament at Christmas. These tournaments encompass darts, dominoes, crib and snooker. Various bowls competitions are also held during the summer months. The snooker table not only provides a source of entertainment for the members, but also on two mornings a week for the Probus Club.

In the summer months the bowling green is used by members and by groups such as the Women's Institute, the Probus Club and also by some of the local British Legion organisations. The green is available for use outside the normal opening hours of the Club. At weekends the Club opens up for use by family groups. Entertainment is provided on most Saturday nights for all, specifically including children. Children have the use of a dedicated play area which includes items such as swings and slides. Older children are encouraged to participate in the various games which are being played by all members, including such events as quiz nights, skittles and karaoke.

A popular feature of the Club's activities is the whist night held every other Monday. Another favourite is the bonfire night party held at the club; all villagers are welcomed to the event, which has proved to be a most enjoyable one over many years.

THE FITNESS LEAGUE

The Hampton Fitness League class started in September 1999 and after the first six months membership stood at over 20. It is affiliated to the National League (originally the Women's League of Health and Beauty), which has over 14,000 members in 300 centres in the UK. This relates back to the Women's League of Health and Beauty founded in 1930. The group meets every Tuesday morning during term time in the Fentham Hall from 10 till 11:45. During the first one-and-a-quarter hours there is a general health and fitness class, and the rest of the session is devoted to those who wish to study movement in more depth and learn sequences. Classes, available to all ages and abilities, consist of exercises designed to tone, stretch and strengthen muscles and improve breathing and joint mobility, so ensuring good all-round health and well-being. Positive posture is at the heart of the approach to health and fitness and is the central pivot from which all movement stems.

The Fitness League in the Fentham Hall – Jane Jennens leads the group.

The Hampton class has quickly become a sociable, fun weekly event, offering safe and effective exercise. Visitors and new members always receive a warm welcome and can be assured of going home feeling uplifted in mind and body.

THE FOLK DANCE GROUP

The roots of the Folk Dance Group were established in the mid-1950s, when the then boot and shoe repairer working and living in the village started to run regular square dances in the Fentham Hall. To ensure good attendance he laid on a coach to run from the centre of Birmingham to Hampton to pick up dancers.

These monthly dances, September to May, have continued without interruption ever since.

From the later 50s to the early 60s a regular weekly youth folk dance group met in the old girls' school. At its peak there were 60-plus registered members. Most of the members were village youngsters, but a significant number came from Solihull, Sheldon, Balsall Common, Meriden and Marston Green. This group of dancers swelled the attendance at the monthly gatherings, making it a successful venture, and a major venue in the world of folk dancing. Hampton folk dances are still a Mecca for devotees, although youthful faces might have aged!

In the early days the American style *square format* dance with singing call was the favourite; now dancers have a very wide repertoire, covering the whole range of folk dance from English Playford to American Contras. The group has always had affiliations with The English Folk Dance & Song Society, who maintain a continued interest and promotion of heritage in folk dance and song.

All dances at Hampton are to live music provided by a number of visiting bands and callers. It is this variation that maintains Hampton as a desirable venue, not only for the dancers but also for the callers and musicians that love to play here.

This does have a down side. Because of its success in the folk world, Hampton has become a little elitist and does not seemingly make it easy for the newcomer to feel comfortable within this experienced company. To that end an associated folk dance club (*The Annex*) meets in the hall of the Methodist Church, Meriden, to provide a venue for the beginner and improver. This club, run by a member of the committee that organises the Hampton dances, has a strong following. It also has visiting callers with a variation of styles and dances to maintain interest.

So that's how Hampton Folk Dance Group appears in the year 2000: the traditional dance still surviving, although other dance crazes come and go. Whether Hampton continues as a centre for community folk dance will, no doubt, depend on the interest shown by the younger generation. There was a time when folk dancing appeared strongly in the school curriculum and every university had a folk dance group. Sadly this is not now so.

Folk Dance Group – Kimberley Smith calls the Dance, "Ad Hoc" plays the music.

THE GARDENING CLUB

The Gardening Club was eleven years old in 1999. It has well over 100 members, 80% of whom live in Hampton.

The Club year has something of the inevitability of the seasons about it. It consists of meetings in the Church Hall, outings and garden visits, special events like competitions and parties, and sometimes open garden weekends. This year was much the same, with the innovation of a Club holiday, but with no open gardens day.

The Church Hall monthly meetings saw 60-70 members and guests squashed in to hear talks on a range of topics, including *Restoration of the Master's Garden at the Lord Leycester Hospital in Warwick* and *Bees in Your Garden*. The quality of speakers varied: those mentioned were two of the best. The day outing in July took 45 members to two gardens in Cheshire. Stonyford Cottage Garden had a splendid nursery, full of good plants at competitive prices. The main destination, the gardens at Arley Hall near Northwich, was judged to be among the best ever seen and members have seen some gardens!

Gardening Club – a summer evening meeting.

The evening outing in June was to the Hiller Garden and Dunnington Heath Farm near Alcester. This time 49 members and friends poured into the private farm garden – which was much admired – and were then conducted in two groups around the Hiller Garden – a very interesting demonstration garden. The plant centre was plundered and supper at the Broom Tavern rounded off the evening.

In 1999 the Club's summer party began at Ann Taylor's Old Farm, with drinks and a viewing of the lovely garden, and moved on to Scotsdale, the home of her mother, Bunty Taylor. It rained.

There was a good field for the Madge Bamber Plate at the annual competition in March for flowers grown or growing from bulbs. Madge Jelph's Clivia Miniata won.

The Stan Bamber trophy is always competed for in July and is judged by Tristan Thacker, who has words of praise and encouragement for every entry, even if only *what a nice pot.* John and Valerie Cook's vegetables and herbs carried off the cup. The last competition, in September was for a single rose. Members *rose* splendidly to the challenge and President Oliver Suffield triumphed.

In early June, 31 people spent four days together in Kent and East Sussex, visiting seven gardens with four houses and a tower. The gardens were splendid, the weather was generally kind, travel was comfortable, accommodation was reasonable and the *esprit de corps* was second to none.

The year ended like all gardening years – looking forward.

Gardening Club – A meeting in the Church Hall – from left – John Trumper, David Shepherd, Raymond Warner, Angela Jones, Maureen Warner, Audrey Wells, Philippa Willetts, Felicity Biddle, Margaret Roberts and Nick Barnett.

HAMPTON COMMUNITY CRAFTS

What more relevant class for the Millennium could there be than one for the making of Millennium Masks (for use at Millennium balls and parties)? A group of ladies assembled in the autumn of 1999 to make masks, and their products have been spied in the window of the Corner Shop as the old century changes into the new. The Arts and Crafts year crosses the line from one millennium to the next, but students are on holiday for Christmas and the New Year. Those who worked hard at craft classes in the autumn term will now be enjoying the fruits of their labours – tassels and cords, hanging baskets, beautiful crafted work of calligraphy, greetings cards, table and flower decorations, items of woodwork (properly turned), silk scarves, mini mohair bears, renovated upholstery work, paintings and drawings and other objects. No doubt some people will be reliving the music of Elgar and his contemporaries which they studied in the autumn. Others might be fighting again the hundred Years War which was central to the literature studies of the dying year, or even engaging in the battles of Ted Hughes and Sylvia Plath. Hampton Community Crafts helps to keep people trim by providing yoga classes. Students should be fit and well, brimful of new ideas for the new century. From the special workshops early in the new year participants will come away with fine photographs, painted glasswork, jewellery, picture frames and high spirits.

There are also days in which many villagers will be collecting together items of interest and value in preparation for an auction of artefacts in the spring, or preparing to attend classes which will help them to make their own videos. Most of the autumn classes have again been on offer from January 2000.

And where is all this done? Mainly in the Arden Room of the Fentham Hall and in the Church Hall. Great support is afforded by the Fentham Trust and the Church. And who are the participants? – a hundred people from the village and a hundred and fifty from neighbouring communities. Do they produce lovely things? Judging from displays in October and December they certainly do. The homes around Hampton must be festooned with numerous craft items from Hampton Community Craft endeavour. Twenty teachers, ten committee members and many bridge players will have enjoyed festive fare confident that they have helped and participated in this productive and life-enhancing operation.

An advanced art session in the Arden Room.

Hampton Community Crafts – In the woodworking room. . . .

. . . . in The Portraiture Class. . . .

. . . . and in the The Upholstery Class.

THE HAMPTON HAS BEENS

Well might you ask what such a title means! To be a *Has Been* you have to have very specific qualifications: namely to be an ex-member of many committees and to have a sense of humour. (With a tag like that you need one!)

A long time ago there was a *Young Wives* club in the village which became *Hampton Wives*. Some committee members endured it for so long that they got quite fond of one another's company, comradeship, wit, conversation and other abilities! In short, they became firm friends and when *Hampton Wives* disbanded they decided to continue to meet as a group, each person to take responsibility to arrange something each month, from *plate and wine*, trips to the theatre, London, weekends and holidays, with the odd *charity do* thrown in (proceeds to Motor Neurone Disease Association, Edwards Trust, Family Unit Trust and others).

There are eleven members who for the new year donned posh frocks and celebrated in style with their partners *The Old Crocs* and friends at 62 Meriden Road: champagne and salmon; balloons and dancing. Festivities lasted into the following afternoon, with a short break to catch breath. Then, eight *Has Beens* and eight *Old Crocs* travelled to Manchester and flew away to Goa in India for a fabulous two weeks' holiday; and yes, all are still firm friends

The Hampton Has Beens are welcomed to Goa from left Mary Sutton, Sue Grantham, Jackie Stanley, Marylyn Elkins, Mike Elkins, Ed Osmund, Mike Grantham, Trish Bell, Terry Barnett, Ray Barnett and Ann James, in front Brian Stanley.

Currently the members are Terry Barnett, Kate Beaty, Trish Bell, Marylyn Elkins, Sue Grantham, Shell Hashemi, Sue Hill, Ann James, Jackie Stanley, Mary Sutton and Marianne Tomlinson.

The Hampton Has Beens Millennium party at 62 Meriden Road (home of Terry and Ray Barnett) from left Sue Hill, Mary Sutton, Shell Hashemi, Trish Bell, Marylyn Elkins, Ann James, Marianne Tomlinson and Sue Grantham. In front Terry Barnett and Jackie Stanley.

THE HAMPTON SOCIETY

First of all, what is it? At a formal level the Society is an Amenity body, affiliated to the Civic Trust. One of its strengths is its large membership, which indicates the level of support in Hampton for its aim, which is *to maintain the character of the village and its environs.*

The Society was formed in 1968 when Hampton was still in Warwickshire. **Some large houses such as Fiddlers Green on Old Station Road and local landmarks such as Sparrow Barracks and the Cattle Market (Fentham Road) had already been demolished for new 'developments'. Meadow Drive had replaced a meadow... and Birmingham thought it would like to draw Hampton into its boundaries. The writing was on the wall!** Concerned villagers were becoming increasingly conscious that the village was situated in a very vulnerable area, and that its rural character was under threat.

At that time Hampton was described as being in a *transitional period.* Since then, having become part of Solihull and with the NEC, Airport and M42 as just the most conspicuous signs of a huge amount of *development,* how best to describe the present village status and the Society's role within it?

The Hampton Society – On the May Day walk to Barston.

The Society tries hard not to conform to the stereotype *Nimby*, but inevitably expends a lot of energy on planning concerns. This is particularly so now that most of the village is *inset* and no longer enjoys the fuller protection of Green Belt status.

Whilst, as with most organisations, the real work of the Society is carried out by an Executive Committee, the full scope of the Society is seen in its sub-groups planning, transport, nature conservation, local history and involvement with arts & crafts. These activities draw in a much wider group of interested villagers.

Light relief is provided for members with the social events in the calendar: a walk on May Day to one of the neighbouring villages, talks on topics of local interest, an annual supper with guest speaker, a bric-a-brac sale; and last year a family day taking photographs as preparation for the Village Design Statement.

Those who established the Society back in 1968 (some of whom are still active in village affairs) did so because they wanted to protect the village from suburbanisation, to preserve something of its rural character and to enhance the special qualities of community life in Hampton.

Since the formation of the Society there has been much change in Hampton and in the beleaguered Green Belt that surrounds it; but there is still much that makes Hampton dear to its inhabitants and desirable in estate agents' terms!

Hampton Society Barbeque – from left – Frances Linn, Malcolm Owen and George Smith.

THE HAMPTON SOCIETY – CONSERVATION GROUP

The Conservation Group set up in 1992 by the Hampton-in-Arden Society had then, as now, a main task of 'managing' the Spinney in Shadowbrook Lane as a local amenity, and for the benefit of wildlife.

This it does on behalf of the owners, Hampton-in-Arden Parish Council, to a plan formulated by the Warwickshire Wildlife Trust.

Additionally the group manages for the George Fentham Trust a piece of land adjacent to the Spinney that consists of two ponds bordered by a small area of uncultivated ground. The group works to a base plan provided by the Ecology Department, Warwickshire County Council.

Both of these areas have benefited from the work of the group.

In the Spinney paths have been defined, overgrown saplings removed, and specific sections cleared of vegetation to allow more light to reach the floor of the wood, the results of which mean less trampling by walkers and the appearance of flora not seen in the wood for many years.

It is expected that with more flowers more insects will move in, which will quite naturally encourage more birds to frequent the area.

The ponds had to be cleared of huge amounts of scrap metal, tyres, wood and other rubbish deposited by farmers and fly tippers over many years. The bordering land had to be cleared of a copse of ash saplings. This area is now rich in wild flowers.

There has also been some tree and shrub planting in memory of a local botanist, Miss Sheila Apted. It is now known to the group as the *Apted Reserve*.

The Hampton Society Conservation Group – working party in the spinney.

It is the group's long-term wish that adjacent arable land should be taken in to increase the reserve to a really worthwhile area of variable habitat for wildlife.

Currently the task of the group is the continued maintenance of the work initially carried out in the 1990s.

It is cxpcctcd that thc Parish Council will soon provide an updated management plan. This will almost certainly involve further sapling removal and tree and understorey planting to ensure continuance of this small but valuable area of woodland.

The Hampton Society Conservation Group – the much improved pond on the far edge of the spinney. (The Sheila Apted Reserve)

THE HAMPTON SOCIETY – THE LOCAL HISTORY GROUP

The Local History Group was started as a sub-committee of the Hampton Society with the aim of providing background information about the history of the buildings in the village in order to assist the planning sub-committee when controversial planning applications were under consideration. However, it soon became a group interested in local history in general, and Hampton local history in particular. One of its objectives is to enable village residents to become aware of the history of their village, and members of the group have given a number of talks on specific aspects of village life to several organisations. The very first presentation was a public lecture given in the Library on the subject of 'Village Shops'. Subsequent topics have included 'Hampton in the 1950s' given to the WI, 'Hampton Manor', a talk sponsored by the Society and given in the green drawing room at the Manor courtesy of Mr John Wood, and a talk on the Public Houses of Hampton given in the Arden Room in Fentham Hall as part of the Society's social programme.

Local historians want to record information about present day activities for the benefit of future generations. In 1993 the group ran a competition, inviting village organisations to produce a display depicting their activities. The entries were judged by Mrs Sue Bates, the Local Studies Librarian with Solihull Central Library, and the Hampton Singers were the winners. There was also a themed category for individuals; the submission by Mrs Pamela Parker was excellent; it recorded the weddings that had taken place during 1993.

The decision to produce the Millennium Book is a direct follow-on from the 'Hampton in 1993' competition.

The group regularly produces displays on varying topics, and these are mounted in Hampton Heritage Centre (also known as the Tearoom) attached to the old Bakery. The space is limited, but the group has been able to display a few artefacts, and a very large number of postcards from the period of the early 1900s up to the 1930s; these two categories form the basis of most of displays. It is believed that during this period Hampton was a very popular place to visit on days out, and thus there were a large number of souvenir postcards available.

The group encourages individual research projects.

THE GEORGE FENTHAM ENDOWED SCHOOL PARENT TEACHERS ASSOCIATION

The Parent-Teacher Association at George Fentham School has been in existence for over 50 years as a non-political organisation aiming to foster close co-operation between parents and staff at the School, and to serve the educational interests of all the children in the School. Membership of the Association is made up of all teachers, Governors and parents of children who attend the School.

The PTA Christmas Fair in the School Hall.

In practice, the main work of the PTA tends to be the raising of funds to contribute towards the purchase of additional equipment and activities (above that which is available from standard funding) within the School.

A committee of 10-15 PTA members organises a schedule of events throughout the school year, the continual challenge being to provide some continuity of events and yet at the same time to have an element of variety in the programme.

In January 1999 Burns Night was celebrated with a supper at the Fentham Hall: after being welcomed by pipers, guests heard Mr Malcolm James (of Corner Shop fame) address the haggis. They then consumed the delicious meal of haggis, neeps and tatties. All this was followed by dancing to the Bedcote Ceilidh Band.

At the end of March there was an Auction of Promises in the School Hall, and the auctioneer (Mr Malcolm Hawksford) was the star turn. The 100 lots were knocked out in record time to an enthusiastic audience, who paused only to demolish a supper of *paté* and assorted cheeses with French bread.

Towards the end of May there was the sale of bedding plants at School, when Caldicott's Nursery of Widney Manor supplied a wide variety of summer bedding plants for sale to PTA members and other villagers.

The end-of-school-year event in July, which traditionally follows on after the School Sports Day, was the Summer Fair, which took place on a wonderfully warm and sunny evening. Baked potatoes and a barbeque were provided, together with a live band which played a fairly mellow selection of jazz and blues numbers. Amusements for the children included the 'Cresta Run' bouncy castles, face painting and a toy stall.

Yvonne Jones ran the tombola stall.

The final PTA event of 1999 was the Christmas Fair, held in early December. The tombola stall was highly popular (as usual) and the cake stall and second-hand toy stalls were very busy. Santa was visited by over 100 children (who were all adamant that behaviour over the last 12 months had been very good). There were stalls selling preserves, Christmas wreaths and books, and it was also possible to purchase a George Fentham Millennium tea towel featuring pen pictures of all the children in the school. The refreshments included hot dogs and hot pork and stuffing baps, which both proved highly popular.

THE HAMPTON PLAYERS

The Hampton Players are the local Amateur Dramatic Group consisting of local people of various ages. To celebrate the end of the Millennium the Players staged a *Theatrical Extravaganza* to show the versatility of the group: it was the first production in a long time which used all the members.

This consisted of a Drama: *The Mansion House Murder*; Shakespeare: *Julius & Cleopatra*; and a pantomime: *Little Red Whittington*.

The Mansion House Murder was written by a member, and portrayed the trials and tribulations of a local drama group putting on a 1930s murder mystery play. *Julius & Cleopatra* told the story of Julius Caesar, the Great Roman Emperor, and Cleopatra, Queen of Egypt. It comically revealed how they got together and how mighty Caesar fell. *Little Red Whittington* was a tale of two pantomime stories: *Little Red Riding Hood* and *Dick Whittington*. It was set in a theatre that had been overbooked and two drama groups turned up on the same night to perform their pantomimes: they decided to merge the two stories, with quite amusing consequences!

Rehearsals began in October 1999 at the Fentham Hall every Tuesday, Thursday and Sunday for five weeks for two hours at a time (depending on how things were going!). The Saturday before the performances all hands assembled to build the sets and to paint the scenery; the lights were put up and the sound system put in place. The following day came the technical rehearsal which enabled the sound engineer, Will Heard, and the lighting director, Tony Worthington, to check that everything was in good working order, and for them to run through their moves.

The production was held on 25, 26 and 27 November 1999 and was a fantastic success, with all tickets sold and rave reviews. It was said by some that it was the *best production for a long while.*

The Players in rehearsal, from left Helen James, Dawn Millard, Erik Yarnell, Nancy Bennett, Coralie Hammond, Chris Sharp, Malcolm James, Janet Allwood, Becky Kear and Des Gershon.

The director was Chris Sharp; stage manager Trish Bell; props mistress Frances Linn; and the cast – Erik Yarnell, Gary Wood, Helen Wood, Harry Smith, Peter Siddall, Coralie Hammond, Nancy Bennett, Rebecca Kear, Selene West, Sarah Cowling, Alexa Bradnock, Laura Doyle, Malcolm James, Nigel Sharp, Des Gershon, Helen James, Dawn Millard, Janet Allwood, Richard Wardle and Macrina Cassey; with thanks to Nick James, Maureen James, Joan Griffiths, and to Yuddi Gershon and Chris Adderley of the Knowle Revels.

Theatre bonanza, from left, Alexa Bradnock, Selene West, Helen Wood, Sarah Cowling, Dawn Millard, Malcolm James, Nancy Bennett, Becky Kear, Harry Smith, Coralie Hammond, Helen James, Janet Allwood, Des Gershon and Laura Doyle.

HAMPTON PRE-SCHOOL

The Hampton-in-Arden Pre-school is open every morning of the week in term time from 9:15 to midday for children between two-and-a-half and five years old. There is one member of staff for every five children, and there are places for 24 children a day at the moment, most of whom come from Hampton and the villages in the immediate vicinity. There are now 34 children who attend regularly, some for one morning a week and some for all five mornings.

At Pre-school the children *learn through play*. Science is popular. Particular favourites are liquid dynamics (or seeing how much of the water activity can be poured on the floor in as short a time as possible), and gravity (what happens when Mrs Kelley trips over an outstretched leg). All this makes a vital contribution to the process of growing up for both children and the staff.

Learning to take part in social activities is a central part of the day at Pre-school. Children love stories, and whilst not all immediately take to sitting down together and being quiet to listen, a good story well read takes some beating. The Vicar seems to score well in this department, but then he has had some practice.

Pre-school in the Scout and Guide Headquarters.

There is a wide range of other activities. The choice is *demand led.* Dressing up from the clothes rail is often demanded by the girls. Riding bikes is demanded by the boys. Sitting quietly watching how to make coffee is regularly demanded by the staff (but rarely happens). Everyone has his or her favourites – Sports Day, the Nature Walk, the Farm visit, and then end-of-year *Prizegiving,* when everyone gets a prize.

The Pre-school is run by a committee of parents whose children attend Pre-school, and they are fortunate to have the support of many others in Hampton. It is extraordinary how many will give up their free time to attend and tell the children about their interesting jobs or strange hobbies. Policemen, firemen, postmen, dentists – even tennis coaches get first-hand experience of crowd control as speakers demonstrate how to clean teeth properly, to breathe using an aqualung or to put out a fire: all absolutely invaluable. Some children are ever so slightly bored and some completely captivated by it all.

The Pre-school is a charity and relies upon fees (currently £4.50 a morning), voluntary donations and fund-raising to pay its overheads. Despite that, and its origins as a playgroup, it is becoming increasingly regulated. There is a *curriculum* which must be followed, the supervisory staff must be qualified, and the Pre-school is inspected once a year to ensure that it is teaching the right things. From 2000 those inspections will be carried out by OFSTED, and the Pre-school will be subject to an additional accreditation procedure by the Local Education Authority and Social Services Department

That the Pre-school can contribute to the well-being of the village children is largely due to the hard work, support and goodwill of those who live and work in the village.

THE PROBUS CLUB

Probus, a contraction of Professional and Business, is an association of clubs without a central organisation, for retired or semi-retired people. Probus in Hampton is an all-male club, limited to 60 members.

As in any club with members of this age range, a few valued friends have passed away during the year, including the secretary, Geoff Barnett. The Club has had the good fortune to attract several new members.

The AGM, held in July at the White Lion, was followed by a photo session for the scrapbook. The new team was elected under the chairmanship of Mike Bryant.

Meetings are held on the third Monday of each month, and some members take lunch at the White Lion immediately beforehand. Other popular 'optional extras' are the outings and visits.

Essential business reports are dealt with before the day's speaker takes the floor, and interest in the topic always generates probing questions.

During 1999 speakers have chosen as their subjects *The Drug Squad, The Battle of the Bulge, Marathon Running, The Birmingham Police, Architectural Curiosities, Soho*

House, a Pharmacist's Work in the Prison Service, Trekking in the Himalayas by Alan Warren, and *A Planter in Malaya* by John Hedley, both club members.

During the year the club enjoyed visits to the Midland Railway Trust at Ripley, the Houses of Parliament and Hughenden Manor, the Triumph Motorcycle factory, Elmhurst Organic Farm, the JCB factory and Soho House. The Ladies' Day visit was to Waddesdon Manor, and the ladies also accompanied members to Westminster.

The Probus Club – At the AGM, front row from left Cecil Jordan, founder President, Mike Bryant, Chairman, Peter Possart, President. In front Robert Elder, second row from left Alan Warren, Peter Daniel and Tommy Weir. At the back from left Michael Reynell, Harry Sutton and Robin Watkin.

In September, Peter Suckling organised a croquet evening and a golf day was arranged by Frank Earnshaw.

The Probus Plodders, a small walking group, meet each month to tackle footpath and stile, with a stop for a pub lunch on the way.

A small working party, led by James Kirby, regularly clears litter from around the Packhorse Bridge and endeavours to keep the area tidy.

As the full membership, with their ladies, exceeds the capacity of *The Spiral Dive*, Christmas lunch is usually split into two parties, and in 1999 the proceeds from lunch time raffles were donated to the Indian Cyclone Appeal.

The Probus Plodders at the Dog and Hedgehog at Dadlington after walking the battle site of Bosworth Field, from left – Alan Warren, John Cordwell, Harry Woodfield, Trevor Lee, Peter Daniel, John Trumper and Robin Watkin.

THE HAMPTON-IN-ARDEN SCOUTS AND GUIDES SUPPORTERS ASSOCIATION

The Association supports the fantastic work of the leaders and maintains the Headquarters building in Shadowbrook Lane.

The Headquarters is home to the Rainbows, Brownies, Guides, Cubs and Scouts. However it is also used by other groups in the village, from Pre-school to the Bridge Club. These activities provide a valued source of revenue.

The committee includes parents, long term supporters and leaders. An annual BBQ in June, a Summer Fair in July, a Jumble Sale in January and other activities bring in much needed revenue.

Scouts, Guides, Cubs, Brownies and Rainbows outside the Scout and Guide HQ after the Remembrance Day Parade.

1st HAMPTON-IN-ARDEN CUB PACK

Hampton-in-Arden has a thriving cub pack for 18 boys ranging from 8 years to $10^{1}/_{2}$ years. Currently the leader is Mrs Rosemary Chapman who is assisted by Mrs Deborah Bransbury, a unit helper. Other support is provided by a rota of parents. Cubs are part of the Scout Association which serves young people between the ages of 6 years and 25 years. The current uniform includes a green sweatshirt and a maroon and yellow neckerchief for normal meetings supplemented by school trousers and shoes for more formal occasions.

During term time the pack meets weekly on Monday evenings and has a varied programme. Indoor activities include craft, learning about the environment and personal development. In the summer the activities are outdoor based, with campfires, outdoor cooking, building shelters, wide games and hikes.

Cubs use these activities as a basis for their award scheme, which consists of the Membership Award, Cub Scout Award, Adventure Award and Adventure Crest. Each successive award requires a higher level of skill and as the cubs progress through the pack the aim is to obtain all of these badges. In addition to these awards are the activity badges and over the last year the pack has undertaken the following: Road Safety, Community, Cookery and Craft. Cubs can take activity badges individually and one cub is currently doing his Local History Badge.

In the past year, the cubs have been away to a weekend camp at Hatton, spent a day learning new games at Rough Close and visited the pantomime. They have also had the opportunity to take part in the district swimming gala and a district outing to the American Adventure Park.

Within the community cubs have helped with the village spring clean, taken part in church parades and at Christmas they held a Blue Peter Bring and Buy Sale rather than a party. The emphasis is on stretching the mind whilst having fun.

1st Hampton Cubs – Chinese dragon making whilst at camp.

1st HAMPTON SCOUTS

Hampton Scouts take part in standard scout training which encourages boys to develop skills, self-reliance and leadership. Nowhere is this more evident than at scout camp. Here the boys have to look after themselves for seven days under canvas, using basic equipment. They have to be able to pitch a tent correctly and keep it tidy and their kit in order. They have to be able to light wood fires, selecting the appropriate kindling, and storing it, when chopped, in a designated area.

1st Hampton Scouts go climbing.

Scouts have to be able to prepare food in a hygienic manner and to cook the food for their patrol from the menu and the stores issued; then they have to be able to wash and clean up and leave the patrol cooking and eating area tidy.

The programme of activities at camp includes hiking, with exploration for the younger ones.

Scouts undertake construction work such as making a bridge with ropes and spars' and also engage in an orienteering project within the locality, using map and compass. The boys are taught how to construct a bivouac from natural material which is rain proof, and then sleep in it overnight. There is also an activity day, which usually involves a canoeing session and either rock climbing or caving. The camp ends with an inter-patrol cooking competition and songs around the campfire.

1st Hampton Scouts try outdoor cooking.

3rd HAMPTON-in-ARDEN RAINBOWS

Rainbows is a group of girls aged from five to seven years old, who belong to the first stage of the Girl Guide movement. At the age of seven they move to the Brownies and later to Girl Guides.

3rd Hampton Rainbows.

Each Monday evening Rainbows meet for an hour at the Scout and Guide Hut to play games, make things, explore themes, sing songs, embark on trips, and have fun: all following the Guiding principles.

1st HAMPTON-in-ARDEN BROWNIES

There are 24 Brownies in the pack who have lots of fun together. In 1999 the Brownies went swimming, produced a play, walked in Hampton, cooked biscuits and picked strawberries. They sang at Hampton Manor and made simple toys for refugees. Brownies learned about first aid, and took their First Aid Badges. On bonfire night they ate hot dogs and lit sparklers around a camp fire. In the summer they enjoyed a week at Kemerton on the Pack holiday, which included a visit to Tewkesbury by bus and a walk to a farm, as well as an opportunity to learn new crafts.

1st Hampton Brownies on a trip to Tewkesbury with leader Fiona Bubb.

2nd HAMPTON-IN-ARDEN BROWNIES

The year began with a visit to the pantomime, followed by a District "Thinking Day" evening concerning Poland. In the next few weeks the Brownies painted T-shirts, made sweets, arranged flowers and planted bulbs. Among the badges gained have been those called *Safety in the Home, Swimmer, Friend to Animals* and *Journey*. The Brownies wrote prayers for Remembrance Day, went as clowns to Brownie Revels and attended the Advent service at Hampton Church.

2nd Hampton Brownies at the War Memorial service on Remembrance Sunday.

1st HAMPTON-IN-ARDEN GUIDES

The Guide Company has 26 guides and 3 adult leaders. They try to maintain a varied and active programme to cater for all the girls. Early in the year 2000 the Guides performed a pantomime as a fund raising venture. They worked hard making scenery and producing costumes, and served teas during the interval.

The Guides have been washing cars around the village over a 6 week period. As a result they have managed to raise £350.

The reason for the fund-raising is to support two guides who have been selected for International camps during the summer of 2000. Abigail Bubb will be visiting Russia and Sarah Chapman is going to Canada.

Later in the year Guides will be going on a Division Camp to Stourport-on-Severn; other plans include making and erecting nesting boxes for birds, outdoor cooking, badge work, a treasure hunt around the village, a family quiz – and above all seeking enjoyment whilst pursuing the guiding programme.

1st Hampton Guides – front row from left – Rose Kiely, Heather Williams, Charlotte Finch, Emma Morris, Charlie Smith, Katie Hands and Teresa Hunt.
Second row from left – Megan Shaw, Sarah Chapman, Kathryn Quigley, Lisa Hollowood, Jenny Cadman and Sophie Kelly.
Third row from left – Elizabeth Read, Carrie Hall, Gloria Hill, Julie Williamson, Eve Jenner, Claire Heffernan and Rachel Cooper.
Back row from left – Frances Kondrat, Stacey Thomas, Michelle Whalen, Alicia Luther Jones, Carly Tropman and Lucy Porter.

THE HAMPTON SINGERS

The Hampton Singers were formed in 1980 to perform the Messiah at the end of the year of celebrations for the 850th Anniversary of the founding of the village church. Members enjoyed singing so much that it was decided to carry on and not disband as had been the original intention.

The Singers, about 35 in number, usually perform two or three concerts a year, and 1999 was no exception.

The Hampton Singers in concert – front row from left – Jean Hill, Vickey Cardwell, Hilary Crosby,
Patsy Priestman, Andrew Dicks, Thelma Borley, Ann Boulter, Jill Briggs and Christine Cook.
Second row from left – Helen Roper, Sue Kiely, Betty Rackham, Ursula Smyth, Les Smith, Lesley Eno,
Pauline Oram, Helen James and Betty Blennerhassett.
Third row from left – Marjorie Douglas, Sandy Wasse, Di Smith, Ted Howarth, Michael Gough,
David Bixby, Bernice Griffiths, Glenys Lamb and Sue Nosworthy.
Back row from left – Ivan Manders, John Trumper, Alan Smyth, Tony Worthington, George Thorpe,
Brian Robinson, Michael Wells and Kit Edwards.

A mixed programme of songs was given to the Solihull Over 50 Club in April. In May the Singers performed Elgar's *From the Bavarian Highlands* and the *Sprig of Thyme*, a selection of well-known folk songs arranged by John Rutter. This programme was shared with the Arden Junior Singers conducted by Janice Greaves, who sang a selection of songs with great professionalism.

In December the Singers presented *Hear My Prayer*, a selection of sacred music, including Mendelssohn's *Hear My Prayer* and Schubert's *Mass in G*; and the Millennium Concert in 2000 was a performance of Haydn's *Creation*.

The Hampton Singers in rehearsal with conductor Andrew Dicks.

TAP DANCING CLASS

At the start of the new millennium Jackie Stanley and all her students – young ones and adults – were all on holiday, taking a well-earned rest from school, work and dancing.

The new term started in earnest in late January – all holidays now over.

Jackie, with the help of Eileen Worthington and Kate Beaty (not forgetting musical accompaniment from Eric Yarnell) began coaching the children with their parts for the concert to be performed at the Meriden Village Hall on Friday 24 March 2000 where Thumberlina, Red Riding Hood, Cinderella, Sleeping Beauty, Pinocchio, Dorothy, Peter Pan and Aladdin (not forgetting Jack and Jill and Dick Whittington) strutted out in style with the leggy lovelies from the 'big girls' class. 'Anything goes' in tap dance land: that is if you know how to shuffle ball change! Classes are held on Monday nights at the Church Hall, and participants can be sure of hard work and lots of fun.

THE HAMPTON-IN-ARDEN WINE SOCIETY

The Society was started in October 1997 at a time when wine-drinking in the UK was at an all-time high and interest in the subject was popular. In addition to the traditional sources in Europe, wines were available from many countries, including New Zealand, Australia, North and South America, Bulgaria, Hungary and more. For day-to-day drinking wine at around £4 a bottle was about the norm, and for special occasions perhaps up to about £20. There were of course those in the world like oil sheiks and pop stars who would pay anything up to £800 for a bottle of Romanee Conti or £2000 for Petrus Pomerol.

The Wine Society Christmas meeting, at nearest table from left Peter Daniel, Hazel Daniel and Michael Reynell. Visiting speaker is Pierre Henck.

The first committee of the Society, with Tom Haig – a Chevalier de Tastevin – as chairman, decided to restrict membership to 36. Initially the participants were mainly husband-and-wife teams. Each member was provided with two tasting glasses to be brought to each meeting. There were to be four meetings a year.

The first meeting was held in the Church Hall in January 1998: a talk on French wines was given by the Chairman. Six wines were tasted, followed by a light supper provided by the ladies of the committee. This became the regular routine for the meetings, and in its first two years outside speakers dealt with wines from South Africa, Australia, France, Italy and England. There was a special event on *Beaujolais Night*, and a day trip to Three Choirs Vineyard and to a Cider Mill nearby also took place.

The meetings were all successful, but perhaps the most auspicious was the AGM/Millennium function in January 2000, when the members themselves were the speakers.

THE HAMPTON-IN-ARDEN WOMEN'S INSTITUTE

Hampton-in-Arden WI celebrated its 80th birthday in May 1999 in recognition of its foundation on 31 May 1919 in a room at the then Ring of Bells pub in the High Street.

The movement then had approximately 100 local members; it developed individual skills and talents so that it grew into one of the leading voluntary organisations in the village today.

A WI Strawberry tea, from left Margaret Possart, Moira Kyles, Geraldine Lee, Betty Jones, Bessie Earnshaw and Maude Craig. In background Mary Weir seated and Doreen Trumper and Ann Smith.

The 1999 programme of fortnightly meetings (with just one in June, July and December and none in August) differs little from previous patterns, the first highlight being the annual Supper Dance in the Fentham Hall in February. Other annuals include a Strawberry Tea in a member's garden, and latterly the challenge to the Probus Club to a game of skittles in Fentham Hall and a bowls match in the grounds of the Fentham Club.

Speakers cover a wide variety of subjects, many illustrated with slides. Members visited the Assay Office in Birmingham, made an afternoon visit to Castle Bromwich Hall Gardens, and booked tickets to see a show written by local comedian Malcolm Stent (*Go and Play up Your Own End*) at Birmingham Hippodrome. Other popular local activities are the weekly table tennis gathering at the Scout and Guide Headquarters, monthly Scrabble evenings and, for hardy outdoors members, walking.

At the annual WI dinner dance in the Fentham Hall.

The West Midlands Federation of Women's Institutes publishes a monthly newsletter – *Cog in the Tree* – with news from other WIs and a programme full of crafts, outings and sporting activities. Darts, Scrabble, Croquet, Petanque and outings have attracted members of Hampton WI, and in 1999 awards were presented to Kay Dearden and Thelma Borley for Scrabble and for croquet.

Hampton-in-Arden WI joins four neighbouring Institutes for a Group Organisation afternoon meeting, providing a friendly link to hear a speaker and indulge in tea and cakes afterwards.

Two bursaries are awarded each year towards the cost of courses at Denman College, the WI residential adult education college at Marcham, Oxfordshire.

The most challenging project of the year was to enter into the West Midland National Federation *Craft Spectacular* where sixty different crafts were approved for entry into five different classes. Hampton-in-Arden WI contributed to Traditional Crafts – namely that of Corn Dolly Making – which was created by Kay Dearden, and arranged on a hand-embroidered tablecloth.

WI table tennis in the Scout and Guide HQ (yes men are allowed!) from left Kay Dearden, Michael Watts, Nora Watts, John Downing, Mary Downing, Peter Daniel, Ann Smith, David Hill, Vin Griffiths, Jean Cubbage, Hazel Daniel, Peter Cubbage, Maureen Moore and Audrey Wells.

Chapter Three:

Local Businesses

There is a wide range of businesses that operate within the village and which are open to the general public. We have not classified these in any way, but have started at the top of the village opposite the church, travelled down the High Street to the Engine and then reversed our direction and travelled back up Fentham Road. Such a journey covers all the public houses and shops.

In addition to these businesses we have two significant businesses in the Village, Wyckham Blackwell and the Ring of Bells Garage. Wyckham Blackwell are a long established timber products company whose main product is roof trusses for house builders. The Ring of Bells Garage in Solihull Road is described below. It was founded in a building next to the Ring of Bells public house when it was still in operation as a pub. In addition to these there are a number of village-based small mainly one-man businesses which are described at the end of this chapter.

THE CORNER SHOP

The Corner Shop, once known as the Top Shop, is on the corner of High Street and Marsh Lane. It is today run by Malcolm James and his wife Maureen, and it adjoins a small hairdresser's, a bakery and a post office. The church lies across the road.

Fierce competition from the large supermarkets now dominates shopping habits, and there is now a further threat – from the Internet. The Corner Shop has to work hard to resist this competition.

The shop today mostly sells delicatessen products and snack foods or foods of convenience. Freshly cut ham, turkey, pork and beef are popular, as is a selection of cheeses, pork pies, sausage rolls and other savoury products. Locally-made sausage is in demand, as is bacon and free-range eggs. Fruit and vegetables sell well, especially organic vegetables which are grown locally. Whereas nearly all milk was once delivered to the doorstep, most milk sales nowadays are through shops and supermarkets. The Corner Shop sells full-fat milk (mostly to young mums who use this for their children) as well as semi-skimmed (half-fat).

The opening hours are 9am to 6pm, Monday to Saturday.

The Corner Shop is a great favourite with residents. It is a congenial meeting place, where many villagers stop to chat and catch up on all the local news.

In the Corner Shop, Malcolm James serves Mr Cattell.

Deliveries to the shop are made on a daily basis by selected suppliers, all offering the best quality products available. Once or twice a week non-perishable goods like tinned foods or cleaning materials are collected from a cash-and-carry warehouse some twelve miles away.

In winter months logs and coal are available, and in summer plants and flowers are sold in large quantities. The shop acts as a booking office for many village social events, as well as being a collection and distribution point. It has a notice board for information of interest and, most important of all, it has a loyal customer base which hopefully will sustain its future for many years to come.

The Corner Shop deli counters.

NO 1 HAIR

This is a small hairdresser's which is now situated at the top end of the village next to the Corner Shop. It originated in the front room of a house in Station Road many years ago, and moved to its present location when the premises became available. Alison, the owner, is a young hair stylist and she is assisted by one full-time and one part-time staff.

Although only a small business, it is well patronised by the residents of the village, and is very popular for the favourite shampoo, rinse and blow-wave. A weekly shampoo and set for older residents is another very popular service, and children are well catered for.

Hair styles include multi-coloured hair, full curls and completely shaven heads. In modern times almost any style of hair has become acceptable. The old traditional men's hairdressers are fast disappearing, and most ladies' hairdressers now cater for men, including this one; so it is not uncommon for Mrs Jones to be sitting in her curlers next to Mr Brown having *a short back and sides.*

Various hair products are on sale in the shop, with items such as hair spray, shampoos and conditioners being the most popular.

The shop is open Monday to Saturday every week, but closes early on Mondays and Wednesdays.

No 1 Hair – In the salon Alison Bowles and Ann Fletcher.

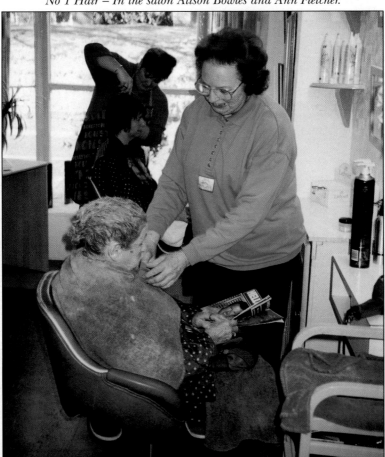

THE OLD BAKERY including NAUGHTY NICK'S SANDWICH BAR AND TEAROOM and the HERITAGE CENTRE

The Old Bakery started some one hundred and fifty years ago, and sold bread and cakes which were baked on the premises – which were then somewhat larger. The bakehouse, ovens, stables and coach house were converted into a bedroom block for the White Lion. Nowadays, because of the arrival of the supermarkets, the demand is no longer there and this, coupled with very strict hygiene regulations, means that those few small bakery shops which remain now buy in stock from larger bakeries. This is done on a daily basis, with hot bread, cakes and savoury products being delivered very early in the morning, ready for the opening of the shop at 8:30am.

To compensate for the loss of traditional trade, this shop has diversified into the making and supplying of sandwiches, both to the village and to local businesses. The sandwich has become the most fashionable lunchtime snack food in this country; hence the arrival of Naughty Nick's Sandwich Bar. This now means that the shop is very busy during the lunchtime period, with sales of crisps and soft drinks running high, and a large selection of sandwiches made to order. However, once this period is over there is no trade and the shop now closes at 2:30pm

Bakery – Nick James at the counter.

The Tea Room is an added bonus to the shop's income because it provides an area where people can sit down for tea, coffee or something to eat. Although small in area, it can seat up to twelve people comfortably and is very popular for early-morning breakfasts, mid-morning tea or coffee and lunchtime snacks. During the summer months, weather permitting, tables and chairs are put out on the forecourt (once the garden) in front of the shop, and these have been a rewarding resting place for many a weary walker or cyclist passing through the village.

The Tea Room, being a central point in the village, is also used as a local Heritage Centre by the village Local History Group. Old photographs and maps are displayed in cabinets around the walls, and are of interest to the captive audience of customers seated at the tables. At regular intervals the Group will put on a display depicting a certain theme. A very popular one was "Hampton during the Second World War".

The Bakery, Christine Clarke and Maureen James.

THE POST OFFICE

Hampton Post Office has undergone some internal re-structuring in recent years. Though the interior space seems a little cramped in comparison with today's modern retailing standards, for many people this adds to the character of the place.

The Post Office, Paul and Gaynor Blackwell.

Most aspects of general postage are covered, with customers being able to post letters and parcels worldwide. Traditional services such as Game & Fishing Licences and Postal Orders continue to be available. A wide range of household bills can be paid, and the office enjoys the status of Motor Vehicle Licence Issuer – something only available at approximately 20 per cent of the post offices in the UK.

On the retail side, a varied selection of newspapers and magazines is available, along with tobacco products, confectionery, stationery and greetings cards. This mix of products attracts a diverse clientele into the shop, from pensioners to young mothers and from businessmen to children. Villagers, employees of the numerous businesses located within the Hampton area and passing trade are also served.

Mornings attract mainly benefit and pension claimants, along with newspaper sales; lunchtimes, office and business workers; afternoons, the *school runs,* and evenings, businesses which drop off post, and evening newspaper sales.

The Post Office network is now under threat as traditional areas of business are threatened. From 2003 the Government is to ensure that all benefit and pensions payments are paid directly into bank accounts. Bill payment is declining from ever-increasing use of direct debit and the rise of the Internet. There is a creeping erosion of the monopoly the Post Office has on delivery services and, indeed, some form of privatisation might be forthcoming after the next general election.

Post Offices are responding to these challenges by moving into new areas such as provision of foreign currency and travel insurance, and by acting as agents for the big banks to try to ensure that everyone in rural areas has access to some form of basic banking service.

The Hampton Post Office remains a key player for many people in the village, offering not only the services mentioned above but, equally importantly, acting along with the other shops in the parade as a focal point for people to meet and exchange news and information on a daily basis.

Hampton Post Office provides a beneficial service for people who cannot or choose not to travel into Solihull to conduct their business and financial activities.

THE WHITE LION

The White Lion pub is open from noon until 11pm for drinks, and provides food and accommodation. Run by John and Linda Moffitt since 1989, it is staffed by fifteen mainly part-time workers.

The small *Front Bar* is the *Regulars'* bar, where both villagers and non-villagers pay frequent visits, generally to drink rather than to eat. *Brew XI* is the most popular bitter and *Carling* the most popular lager.

The White Lion.

The *Front Bar* is a meeting place where friendships are made and renewed, and there is much chat, discussion and gossip. Whilst women are made very welcome, most of the customers are male, the majority being aged between 35 and 55. They have a keen interest in watching sport, enjoying the shared experience of viewing important football or rugby matches on the pub television. Few young drinkers visit the *Front Bar*, preferring to visit theme pubs and bars elsewhere.

The traditional bar is a place where one can always find the right person for any job that needs doing – from plumbing to insurance, gardening, legal advice to buying a new car: there is always some one who does the job or knows some one who does. Pub events are arranged here, especially those connected with raising money for the *White Lion*'s main charity, *Marie Curie Warren Pearl* in Solihull.

The Side Bar of the White Lion.

The larger *Side Bar* also has many regular customers, but is more of a lounge bar with far more seats and tables than the *Front Bar*. During weekday lunchtimes office workers from the village and further afield take their lunch breaks here, which means the room is often very busy from one until two o'clock. Others meet here for a more leisurely lunch, or just for a drink. Walkers and cyclists pop in for a rest and refreshment. At night couples and groups of friends sit and chat. The Hampton Singers and Bellringers come here for drinks after their practice.

Food is served in the Front and Side bars and the Restaurant at lunchtime, when customers can choose from the sandwich, traditional or *a la carte* menus. In the evenings, meals are only served in the *Spiral Dive* restaurant, which can seat up to 50 people. The *a la carte* and *Specials* board provide a wide choice of dishes, and the fresh fish specialities are becoming increasingly popular. The restaurant also caters for weddings, funerals and christenings. Probus holds its monthly afternoon meetings here.

The proximity to Birmingham, and especially its airport and the NEC, keeps the accommodation side of the pub very busy. Bookings for rooms are made up to two years in advance for large shows such as *Crufts* and the *Spring* and Autumn Fairs.

As the new millennium opens, the White Lion is regarded by its customers as being one of the few surviving traditional pubs in the area. Uncluttered by fruit machines and the noise of the juke box, it is at present a place where people meet to talk. The Bed and Breakfast side of the business guarantees that the pub is now visited by people from all over the world, as well as locals and people passing through the village. Many are impressed with the history of the building and with the idea that it has been providing a service to people for so many years.

THE VILLAGE STORES

The Village Stores has been situated at 40 High Street since 1993. The premises are leasehold, comprising the shop and flat above.

The Village Stores.

The majority of customers using the shop are from the village, but strangers have been known to comment "there aren't many shops like this still around!". Many similar shops have long since closed and, in order to retain business, the shop is now open longer hours than in the past, and sells a wider range of goods.

The shop operates as a general store, and is open six days a week. Monday is the rest day, and the shop is open from 10am to 8pm Tuesday; 9am to 8pm Wednesday; 9am to 6pm Thursday; 9am to 8pm Friday and Saturday; and 7:45am to 3pm Sunday. Most of the time only one person is required to serve, though there are occasions when two are needed.

Of the eight categories of products, the line generating the highest takings each week is cigarettes. They bring in about 25% of the weekly takings. Profit margins are small because there is a large element of tax and duty.

Sunday sales of newspapers are the foundation on which the business survives, providing 20% of the week's takings and profit. Sunday is by far the busiest day of the week with over 300 people visiting the store each Sunday, generating 40% of the week's takings. The Mail on Sunday and the Sunday Times are the two best selling titles. A delivery service is available for those who want it, and a reservation service for those wanting to collect the same paper each week. Two people are required to serve throughout the day on Sundays.

Mike Grundy in the Village Stores.

The remainder of the week is managed by Mike Grundy and his partner Diane Hughes, who also runs Hampton Wines.

The volume of fruit and vegetables has been consistently in decline over recent years. The range of stock on offer is now limited to the basics, as stocking the more unusual produce has proved too costly and wasteful. Fruit and vegetables are collected on three occasions each week, mostly from Birmingham wholesale market, requiring a 6:30am start; hence the rest day on Monday and late opening on Tuesday.

Flower sales fluctuate from week to week, making volumes difficult to forecast. As with the fruit and vegetables, they are mainly bought from the Birmingham wholesale market. The prime sellers are chrysanthemums, spray carnations (throughout the year), daffodils and tulips (when in season). Other flowers are only offered to order or on special occasions.

Ice cream sales are a good attraction during the warmer weather. A hot summer can pull in passing trade from customers who would not otherwise use the shop.

The remaining categories are either VATable (pet foods, cleaning products, chocolate products; minerals; personal hygiene products); or non-VATable (cakes, preserves, meat, bread, milk, eggs, tinned and packaged foods). A local farm shop supplies fresh meat, and eggs are delivered by a local free-range chicken farmer.

HAMPTON WINES

Hampton Wines – *The Offie* – is a supplier of beers, wines and spirits to the community and its visitors. Within a small village such as this the Off Licence has more of a community role than its High Street counterparts. Opening hours of lunchtime and evening and all day Friday and Saturday meet with the pattern of village life.

Hampton Wines.

In exceptional circumstances the shop will sell to customers out of normal hours to meet the needs of the village. The main stock items are beers, wines and spirits, complemented by cigarettes, sweets, snacks, nibbles and ice creams; and some essentials (loo roll, toothpaste, batteries, cat/dog food etc) and milk, on behalf of the Village Stores next door when they are closed. Credit and debit card transactions are processed electronically, and Visa, Mastercard, Switch, Solo and Delta cards are accepted, as well as cheques and cash.

Being in a village, there are rarely gangs hanging around with nothing else to do but cause mayhem, as happens in larger shopping areas. Nevertheless modern security is obtained by the installation of a cast iron latticework scroll inside the windows to deter would-be burglars.

The building was constructed in 1868 and is Grade II* listed. The shop's position on the corner of High Street and Butchers Road means that its internal dimensions are unusual, and there is a labyrinth of storerooms in this former butcher's shop.

The owners buy goods and take the risk upon themselves. Every endeavour is made to cater for the special wishes of customers. Efforts are constantly made to compete with supermarkets, and sometimes the store can offer lower prices.

The *Offie* is a delightful and characteristic part of the village.

Diane Hughes serving in Hampton Wines.

THE ENGINE

The Engine has been owned by Bass Leisure Retail for many years. In 1996 it was refurbished into a *Harvester*. The *Harvester* brand is a family restaurant concept with high focus on fresh wholesome food and excellent friendly guest service. The menu includes over thirty different main courses, including chicken, beef and fish and combination platters for two to share.

With all meals on offer you have the chance to visit the famous *Harvester Salad Cart*, which contains more than a dozen different freshly-prepared salad items for you to help yourself.

The entrance to the Engine.

The Engine also offers special discounts to diners at lunch time and in the early evening. There is a *Privilege Guest* scheme which allows the over-55s discounts at most lunch times.

A lot of the trade for the Engine comes from the NEC and local businesses, although it also works closely with guest houses in the village to provide their guests with a welcome meal at the end of a long day. Local families are catered for with a special *Out of This World* menu for children.

The provision of a restaurant and pub for the residents of Hampton-in-Arden helps a lot of the young people from the village by affording them employment. The catering trade has always been an excellent way of financing the way through college, and The Engine Harvester always looks to the community when the need for recruitment arises. Young employees have the opportunity to enrol on a NVQ course while working at the Engine Harvester.

The Engine is a successful restaurant and brings people from the surrounding areas to experience the friendly and welcoming village of Hampton-in-Arden at the beginning of the new century.

Salad Bar and cooking area in the Engine.

LLOYDS PHARMACY

The small, privately-run chemist shop that started out on these premises now belongs to Lloyds, a well-known chain of chemists with over 1,000 shops spread around the country.

It is a dispensing chemist and maintains a close liaison with the village surgery. Not only do people bring their prescriptions to the chemist after a visit to the doctor, but repeat prescription orders may be collected from the surgery by the chemist's staff to be picked up the following day by the patient or representative.

In addition to the dispensing part of the business the pharmacist is also able to give people advice and guidance about medications and ailments.

The shop sells a wide range of proprietary medicines, as well as a range of toiletry products, cosmetics, baby and household products. A next-day service is available for the developing and printing of films.

As you would expect, most residents of the village have been through the door of the pharmacy at some time or another, and most are known by name!

Fentham Road shops – Lloyds Pharmacy, Total Images and Hampton Stationery.

TOTAL IMAGES

Soo Townley and Trish Savidge have been the co-owners of Total Images since 1 February 1999.

A hairdressing service is offered to all the family in a warm and friendly atmosphere. Clients range from six months of age to ladies in their nineties. It is unusual for hair salons to be open on a Monday but this one is open all day (9:30-5:30) Monday to Friday and 8:30-1:30pm on Saturday. Some appointments are even made a little after hours. The products used are by Schwarzkopf – a company of long standing.

The salon at 48 Fentham Road has on one side a chemist and on the other side a printer. The two floors above are offices, let to various businesses. The block is owned by a company called Nattrass Giles, the landlord, based in Birmingham.

The salon looks out onto the old school of Hampton, which is now the village library.

On Monday, Tuesday and Wednesday reduced rates to OAPs are offered. On Saturdays and Wednesdays additional workers are employed.

Total Images – Soo Townley and Trish Savidge.

OMEGA

The present owner, Steve Paggett, moved here in 1987, taking over the lease of a dress shop. They were eighteen months into their lease, but things did not go well for them. A hardware store had been here previously for around twenty years.

The firm is known as *Hampton Stationery*, selling basic stationery etc. The business name is *Omega Design and Print*. This covers all aspects of printing from full colour to business cards. Customers have been attracted over the years ranging from one-man businesses to plcs. Even Japanese companies based in Birmingham and a customer in France make use of Omega's services. Unfortunately Steve does not get to deliver the French lady's printing: she picks it up. The shop also supplies local businesses, including Age Concern in Solihull, for printing, photocopying and faxes; etc.

The firm hopes to be able to serve the people of Hampton for years to come.

RING OF BELLS GARAGE

The Ring of Bells is a Volvo Dealership, selling new and used vehicles, offering service and repair work, body and accident repair work, and a comprehensive parts department. Almost 40 staff are employed, many of whom have been with the company for a number of years.

The Ring of Bells Garage.

John Baker has owned and managed Ring of Bells for 30 years, initially as a Leyland Dealership, transferring to Volvo in 1978.

At the end of the 20th century Shell decided to cease supplying fuels to low volume forecourts such as that of the Ring of Bells. It was decided to discontinue fuel sales, opting for Q8 until planning permission could be obtained to remove the canopy and pumps. The canopy should have disappeared by April 2000 and with it the end of fuel sales from Ring of Bells.

During the autumn of 1999 the motor trade fell victim to two much publicised threats: namely the internet and grey imports. Also the purchase of Volvo by the Ford Motor Company and impending changes to retailing legislation, have added to the company's concerns.

Unsurprisingly Ring of Bells entered the year 2000 rather quietly. Nevertheless the company is experiencing an upturn in business. It is believed that consumers research the market for themselves, and appreciate that Ring of Bells can offer them a very competitive and personally tailored service.

WYCKHAM BLACKWELL

In 1991 a book, 'Trading in Timber', recorded the change in the village-based timber business of Wyckham Blackwell. Founded in 1884 the general timber merchant business changed to become a volume producer of roof trusses for the house building industry. The changes over the last century ensured the continuity of employment and family ownership of the timber based business – a century of great change."

During the past decade the old station buildings have been refurbished and are now listed and a new office block has been built in the proximity of the manufacturing units where computer fed angled cutting was installed in 1997.

A further opportunity arose in 1998 to develop the design and fix of the well established American outdoor living concept 'decking' with the first installation in the garden of a new Bryant home in Meriden Road.

SMALL BUSINESSES

There are a large number of small businesses either run from many of the office buildings within the village or from people's homes. Buildings specially built for offices include Hampton Court in Marsh Lane, Enterprise House and the offices over the shops, both in Fentham Road and the former offices for Wyckham Blackwell in Old Station Road. Buildings originally built for other purposes and now converted into offices include the former Ring of Bells public house on the corner of Belle Vue Terrace and Solihull Road, Church House, formerly Church Farm in Solihull Road and the Old Station in Old Station Road.

One man businesses based in the village which regularly advertise in the Church and Village Chronicle include Church Barn Heating and Plumbing in Solihull Road, L A Quick – Carpentry, Shop Fitting and Builders – in Old Station Road, W Baum – Roofing Contractor, Dove Home Care Agency as well as a local psychotherapy service and a private physiotherapist.

Chapter Four:

Services available in the Village

Compared to most villages local residents have a good range of services available within Hampton-in-Arden. High on the list is the availability of a local doctor, with a supporting chemist located in Fentham Road. Services provided by Solihull Metropolitan Borough Council include a branch library and a refuse collection service. There is a good local railway service to both Birmingham and Coventry and a bus service to Solihull. A wide range of products are delivered, on request to the door and there is still a local bobby.

In addition to those listed there are a number of other services available to residents such as home help services and garden maintenance. Some of the people providing these services are also residents of the village but quite a number come in from outside. In the case of home-helps, a number of mini-buses bring in a regular number every day. There are a number of window cleaners operating in the village, all from outside.

Solihull Metropolitan Borough Council provide home care facilities for the village.

THE HAMPTON SURGERY

The present surgery is a modern building, purpose-built in 1991, with access facilities for disabled people. It is situated on the Fentham Club car park off Marsh Lane. Dr Rodger Charlton succeeded Dr Peter Mace early in 1995 and has enhanced the practice team and services available. Sister Susan Cooper has served for many years as the practice nurse, and currently the support staff includes Mr Colin Macnair, the Practice Manager, and receptionists Mrs Vicky Cardwell, Mrs Carolyn Coverdale and Mrs June Hand.

Most residents of Hampton-in-Arden and others from Bickenhill, Barston, Catherine-de-Barnes and adjacent parts of Knowle and Solihull are patients. Dr Charlton has a special interest in the training of GPs and the practice is recognised as a Training Practice where qualified and experienced hospital doctors undergo a twelve-month's training period before entering practice. They are called GP Registrars.

People in Hampton are fortunate to be able to call upon the services of District Nurses, Midwives, Physiotherapists, Health Visitors and Chiropodists, as well as having a comprehensive emergency service out-of-hours. There are surgeries every weekday morning and afternoon (except Thursday afternoons), and an emergency surgery at Knowle on Saturday mornings. The practice operates an appointments system and home visits are available for those who are housebound or too ill to attend surgery. The following clinics are available: baby immunisation; ante-natal; physiotherapy; warts/minor surgery; diabetes, asthma and family planning.

The Surgery – Dr Helen Liley, Carolyn Coverdale, Vickey Cardwell, Colin Macnair, Sue Cooper, Jackie Bird and Dr Rodger Charlton.

Records are now in A4 folders, in addition to being computerised. Much new medical equipment is available. Some of this has been purchased from the Equipment Fund which is regularly supported by sales of pictures by local artists, raffles, and personal donations by appreciative residents. A cardiac defibrillator has been purchased by the Fentham Trust.

Healthcare in the UK is developing rapidly as a result of technology, consumerist and political forces, and there is a move to centralise care in large hospitals and to amalgamate GP surgeries into large practices. The presence of a solo practice in a village setting is now exceptional for the personal service provided by a single family doctor and associated dedicated healthcare team. This unique situation close to large urban centres should be protected, and this will require the support, input and understanding of local residents/patients, as the existing practice strives hard to maintain this facility.

Outside the Surgery.

THE LIBRARY

At the turn of the century Hampton-in-Arden Library is still a typical village library, with an enthusiastic and well-read clientele. The variety and scope of the material requested by Hampton borrowers is a constant source of surprise and a heartening characteristic in the view of the library staff. It is no wonder that Hampton library is well-known within Solihull village libraries (Hampton, Balsall Common, Marston Green and Meriden) for being the reservation capital of the four. Book stock is limited, but Hampton readers will request anything they want in the knowledge that the items can usually be obtained.

The building itself is relatively unaltered since its days as a school, and this inevitably causes problems when trying to meet the ever-changing demands of the village population. Space is very limited, and because of this there is very little seating and no study areas in the library. Only books and talking books can be borrowed from the library at present, but there is a wide range of information available to borrowers.

The book stock is rotated amongst the village libraries once a year to make the stock work harder and there are collections within the library system which highlight certain areas of stock with displays, such as Booker Prize winners, 60 years of Penguin Books and Graphic Novels, specifically aimed at teenagers.

The children's reading corner in the Library.

It is a certainty that as the new millennium begins, Hampton Library will come to have CD-ROMS and Internet links, bringing further technology into a building which is nearly 200 years old.

There is no typical Hampton borrower. Out of the 570 borrowers currently registered, there is a broad cross-section of adults (young and old), infants and children. However, the Hampton borrower seems to know exactly what he or she wants, and that the library is the place to access this material.

Because the library has only one permanent member of staff, and limited opening hours (Tuesday 9:30-12:30 and 1:30-5:00 and Friday 1:30-5:00 and 5:30-7:00), this impinges upon the amount of work that can be done with outside groups. At the moment there are regular story times for the under fives every other Tuesday between 2:30 and 3:00. There is a visit to Hampton Manor to read and take any books that might be required on a fortnightly basis. Library staff also visit Hampton Pre-school every other Thursday for a story session, and make contact with the George Fentham Nursery Unit every term for stories and a library visit.

Hampton Library is very much part of the community. As ever, in an ideal world, more monetary input would further enhance the service and provide more for the people who currently use Hampton-in-Arden Library, and for future library users.

In addition to the Fentham Road Library the Solihull MBC mobile library visits the village every other week and stops at a number of locations including Fentham Green. The facility is aimed at providing services for people with limited mobility.

The Library – children choose their books.

TRANSPORT

The village lies within the West Midlands conurbation which stretches from Wolverhampton in the north west to Coventry in the south east. The local authorities within this area have formed a consortium company – *Centro* – to provide and co-ordinate public bus and local train services. Free travel is provided throughout the system, at specific times to certain groups of residents, including the elderly and students attending courses.

Historically Hampton has been at the hub of the country's transport system since the bridge was built over the River Blythe in the thirteenth century, to carry pack horses transporting salt from Droitwich to Coventry and beyond. In the eighteenth century the canal system came within two miles of the village, with wharfs at Catherine-de-Barnes and Henwood.

A Taxibus passes the Post Office.

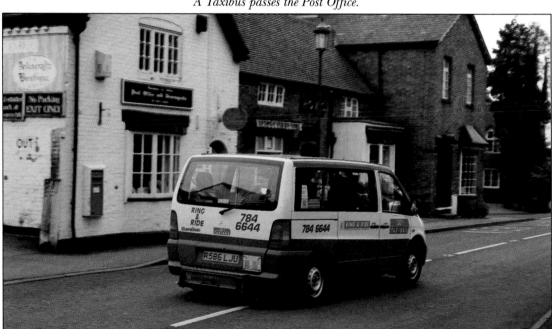

1838 saw the opening of the Birmingham to London railway line. This was followed by the building of a line between Derby and Hampton to enable travellers from Derby to catch the London trains. This was not a success as a line directly from Derby to Birmingham offered a better route. Thus the Hampton junction station was no longer required and a new station was built on the present site. This was later lengthened to cater for the London bound express trains. It was only in the 1970s that the opening of Birmingham International Station caused the direct expresses to stop calling at Hampton.

The station now only offers a half-hourly local service to Coventry in one direction and to Birmingham and Wolverhampton in the other. There is a restricted weekend service.

Commuters boarding the train to Birmingham.

Next to Birmingham International Station is Birmingham International Airport, offering a range of scheduled and of charter flights which cater for summer holiday makers. Birmingham International Station also provides a pick-up point for intercity coaches and coaches to other airports. The village is well placed for access to the M42 via junctions 5 and 6.

On weekdays the village is currently served by bus services to Coventry and to Solihull, at hourly intervals. In addition there are *Ring and Ride* and *Taxibus* services provided by West Midlands Special Needs Transport Ltd through *Centro*. These operate door to door and require 24 hours' notice. Most vehicles are *transit* van size, adapted to take wheelchairs.

Catching the bus to Solihull.

The George Fentham Charity supports the Hampton Community Transport Service. This voluntary service is co-ordinated by Vin Griffith on behalf of the Parish Church, offering elderly and disabled villagers help with essential journeys. Fifteen drivers give their time and the use of their cars; expenses are met by the Trust. On weekdays most pupils are transported by bus to and from schools within the borough, and on Wednesdays Age Concern provides door-to-door transport for those attending their meetings.

Despite these services the car is still the most popular form of transport. Traffic through the village causes problems both in terms of speed and volume. It is estimated that around 1200 cars belong to the 750 dwellings in the village. There are several congestion points and traffic problems are exacerbated by the amount of all-day parking on side roads by employees of local businesses and others.

POSTAL SERVICES

All mail for Hampton-in-Arden, whether posted locally or from more distant locations, is processed in Aston at the new Birmingham Mail Centre, which was opened for service in January 1999. The new Mail Centre marks a significant step forward for the Royal Mail, with new technology playing a vital part in the effective, speedy processing of mail. Six *Integrated Mail Processors (IMPs)* each sorting mail at an average of 27,000 items per hour, make Royal Mail Birmingham the flagship amongst Mail Centres worldwide.

The *IMPs* sort all B90 to B95 coded mail for despatch to Solihull Delivery Office. At Solihull the mail goes through further manual segregation, sorting and allocating the mail to the respective 'B' code delivery offices.

Roger Haddock makes a delivery in Fentham Close.

Khalid Mahmood collects the post from the box at the Post Office.

Mail destined for Hampton-in-Arden is *walk-sorted* at Solihull Delivery Office, meaning that the mail is sorted according to the order in which it is to be delivered. Three postal staff serve the village: two on foot and one on *driving duty*. Hampton-in-Arden receives two deliveries each day Monday to Friday and a single delivery on Saturday.

Domestic mail is collected throughout the day at the times stated on each pillar box. There are five of these pillar boxes in the village: one set in the wall of the Post Office; one set in the wall in Marsh Lane near the junction of Bellemere Road; and one set in a wall in Old Station Road. There is a post box attached to a telegraph pole in Diddington Lane and the only free standing pillar box is at the junction of The Crescent and Meriden Road.

Commercial mail is collected from various firms and businesses, if requested, each working day between 3:30 and 6:00pm.

Mail is collected from the village post office four times each day from Monday to Friday and from two boxes on Sunday. All mail collected from the village is taken to the Solihull Office where it is containerised and sent on to be sorted by the IMP machines at the Birmingham Mail Centre. There is a guarantee that the mail assembled each day is in the Birmingham Centre by that evening for onward delivery.

Improved technology in the sorting and delivering of mail has brought about great changes over the years. In the 1950s and 60s the excess volume of mail in the village each Christmas was delivered, stored and sorted by temporary postal workers in the village Cricket Club pavilion. *Peter the Postman* barricaded himself and the Christmas post inside the building and not even the Cricket Club Chairman was allowed entry. IMPs are very efficient but seem to have taken some of the personal flavour out of village life.

REFUSE COLLECTION SERVICES

The collection of refuse, both domestic and commercial, is controlled by the Director of Environmental Services from the Solihull Metropolitan Borough Council office.

Over the entire borough 81,000 tons of waste are disposed of each year. Sixty per cent is incinerated, thirty four per cent is dry layered on landfill sites which then produces gas to generate power and the remaining six per cent, mainly glass, paper, textiles and metal, is re-cycled. The environmental services are considering ways of increasing the re-cycling percentage in the future by requesting house-holders to separate suitable re-cycling materials prior to collection.

Public waste disposal sites are also available for the free dumping of household materials, large items of furniture and garden refuse. Those people who do not wish, or are unable to deliver waste to the centres, may arrange to have their garden refuse collected. Special pre-paid official sacks are made available for this service.

Two refuse collection rounds operate in Hampton-in-Arden. On Monday each week a vehicle removes and replaces *metal Paladin containers* used as communal refuse bins at all blocks of flats. On Wednesday each week, commencing at 6:30am, a domestic collection vehicle calls at all houses in the village removing refuse placed in bin liners. For each bag collected that day a new bin liner is provided to the householder for the following week's collection. In addition to the normal refuse collection the environmental services teams will collect unwanted cookers, fridges and freezers on request, free of charge, and any other bulky items for a small charge.

All refuse collected from the village and other Solihull areas is transported to the Coventry and Solihull Waste to Energy Plant for final re-cycling in some form to provide energy or for remaking useable items.

Collecting the refuse in Fentham Road at the corner of Butchers Road.

DELIVERIES IN THE VILLAGE

A large number of products are delivered to houses in Hampton including milk and coal from old established roundsmen. As supermarkets expanded and small shops were forced to close, a specialist group of van sales began to develop. Newer delivery rounds include a frozen food delivery service.

Mark delivers milk in Fentham Road.

Fresh fish deliveries are made by Brian Baker, who was born and bred in Grimsby, and has worked all his life in the fishing industry. However, fishing has in recent times suffered badly. When Brian found himself out of work, and saw an advert one day for a delivery round for sale, he decided to have a go. Far from Grimsby and from the coastline though Hampton may be, fresh fish is always in great demand.

Brian delivering fish to Miss Anderson.

Brian's van is specially equipped with ice to keep everything fresh, and can cater for all types of fish. He travels down in the early hours of Wednesday mornings, to arrive at Hampton-in-Arden at about 8am ready for the day's deliveries. He goes from door-to-door with his wares, and most of his customers are regular weekly calls. Having completed his round in Hampton, he travels on to Balsall Common, and then to Meriden, where he stays overnight. The next day he travels to Cheltenham, sells the remainder of his fish there, and then heads back home to Grimsby.

Another example is frozen foods. This is supplied in the area by two companies specialising in large ranges of frozen products designed for the average home freezer. Vegetables, fish and meat products and chips are some of the most popular items.

Frozen food being delivered.

One of the newer rounds in this area delivers pet foods for animals and birds. This is especially helpful to the elderly in the village who keep pets for company but cannot get to the big stores for supplies.

Milk is supplied through large distributors of which there are two in the village, the Co-op and Avonmore Dairies. People can now purchase from their milkman several grocery items, tea, bread, eggs, confectionary and even house plants. Pettifors of Meriden supply coal in this area but modern central heating systems have been the cause of reduced sales of coal. Pettifors now sell logs and sticks and small bags of pre-packed coal to local shops.

Chattaways of Balsall Common must be one of the few traditional ironmongers left in the area and certainly one of the last still to offer a van sales service. He covers all the local farms and elderly residents in Fentham Green and

Mr Chattaway at Fentham Green.

Delivering in Marsh Lane.

Wellmeadow Grove. The van carries a wide range of hardware items ranging from brushes to light bulbs.

Since the delivery of parcels was privatised a number of companies have been set up to deliver parcels not just locally but worldwide. Several serve the village including Parcel Force, White Arrow and D.H.L. All offer a 24 hour service to the door but not all quite make it.

The Mobile Library at Fentham Green.

Finally Tesco, the supermarket chain recently started an online shopping via the internet, Tesco Direct, with doorstep delivery. The first sighting of this in the village was very recent but, unfortunately, the customer was not at home for this delivery.

POLICING

Policing in the West Midlands went through many changes prior to the turn of this century. The introduction of sector policing in 1999 changed the role of the *village bobby*. Previously the village policeman (PC Malcolm Milner at the time of the change) was solely responsible for all aspects of policing within the village of Hampton. The village police officer lived in the police house in Diddington Lane, which had its own office where the villagers could go. The village was, in fact, this officer's *beat*. He was also responsible for other smaller villages surrounding the parish such as Barston, Bickenhill and Catherine de Barnes.

Sector policing was designed to improve the service provided by the police to the residents of Hampton. The police officer remained in residence in the village at the police house, and the office was still manned. The village police officer still had the responsibility for Hampton as a village, but also he became part of the sector that covered a larger rural area which incorporated Balsall Common, Meriden and Berkswell. This change took place to increase police cover to all rural areas, carried out by increased numbers of police officers, which meant Hampton could be policed in the absence of the *village bobby*.

Sector policing also enabled the police to become more involved in crime prevention measures, and to liaise with residents about crime trends in the area through Neighbourhood Watch. The police now consult with the local council about issues that affect village people, such as better street lighting and road safety issues.

Policing may have changed but Hampton-in-Arden still retains a resident *policeman*.

OTHER SERVICES

A number of services are provided by and for village residents. The church takes a lead in welcoming all newcomers to Hampton. A small group of visitors, co-ordinated by Flix Haynes, delivers a 'welcome pack' of useful village information soon after newcomers move in. This is followed by a welcome in the 'Chronicle' and, once a year, a newcomers tea in the church hall when the newly arrived can mix socially with established residents.

A quarterly lunch for the senior members of the village, the Over 65s lunch, started in 1987 following a discussion between some of the "older" young wives who felt that they would like to do something to benefit residents of the village. It was started by Angela Jones, Jean Cubbage and Roslyn Ellender who felt that there were villagers who lived alone and wouid probably welcome the opportunity to join with others for the occasional meal. Accordingly an invitation was placed in the Church & Village Chronicle and on the 18th March 1987 some 24 residents met in the Church Hall for the first lunch, this has now grown to approximately 50 who sit down to a three-course lunch at tables decorated with fresh flower arrangements created by Mary Weir and now held in The Arden Room at The Fentham Hall to accommodate the increased numbers.

It is not just a lunch but a social occasion which is very much looked forward to by everyone. The participants enjoy the time in the company of members of their own generation and are very appreciative of the good food and helpful service provided.

After the meal the helpers, all volunteers, join Angela, Jean and Roslyn for their own social event when they sit down to their lunch.

A village telephone book is produced every few years which is an extract from the Birmingham South East telephone directory and is a must in a large number of village homes. It is much more convenient than the large tome produced by British Telecom. On a slightly less frequent basis a Village Handbook is produced listing contacts for all village organisations. This was a separate publication but recently has appeared as a supplement to the Church and Village Chronicle. But again another very useful reference book for residents. Both publications are the work of Mary Owen and all profits go to the parish church.

Chapter Five:

Sporting activities within the Village

THE HAMPTON-IN-ARDEN BADMINTON CLUB

Records indicate that the Hampton-in-Arden Badminton Club was founded in 1949 under the chairmanship of Paul Randall.

Initially the court must have been marked out on the floor, because in 1954/55 a badminton mat was bought. This would have entailed unrolling the mat and rolling up after each club meeting, to be stored at the back of the hall, as still happens.

Membership gradually increased over the years to a peak of about 40. Play took place on three evenings and two afternoons each week, with one evening being reserved for matches against other clubs, as friendlies and league games.

In 1987 a junior section was formed, but was dissolved in 1990, when most of the older members left for further education, and there was lack of support.

The club was affiliated to the All England Badminton Association and was very successful in competition. For instance, in 1983 the ladies' team won

The Badminton Club in Fentham Hall.

Division 1 in the Solihull League. Success in the various leagues continued right up to 1989. Sadly this was the last time Hampton-in-Arden appeared in the league tables, as the league players merged with the Arden Club in Knowle.

The club starts the new millennium with a total membership of 18 players, but is looking to increase this number during the course of the year. Play takes place on Monday evening from 7pm (mixed) and on Thursday afternoon from 2pm (ladies).

The group has been fortunate in replacing equipment with new up-to-date items, such as a blue mat, which is cushioned and gives a firm hold and minimum stress on muscles and joints. Also there are new posts with built-in weights and wheels for easy movement. This has been possible with substantial assistance from the George Fentham Trust.

THE HAMPTON-IN-ARDEN CRICKET CLUB

Hampton-in-Arden Cricket Club is an integral part of the social and sporting life of the village. At its present location at Corbett Field in the heart of the village, cricket is enjoyed and watched at one of the most picturesque locations in the *heart of the Midlands* and in one of the oldest clubhouses in England, if not the world! Hampton-in-Arden Cricket Club was established in 1860 and cricket has been played over the years at various locations around the village. The Club was re-established in 1948, so that in 1998 the Club celebrated its Golden Jubilee at Corbett Field.

As the new millennium dawns, Hampton-in-Arden CC has achieved for the first time in its history promotion to the Birmingham & District Premier League, having won the Warwickshire Division One Cricket League. This was a proud achievement for the club and for players, members and supporters. It was the result of home-grown development of boys living in the village joining with players from outside the village but within the Solihull Area. *The Hampton Lions*, a junior team, has attracted boys and girls in the village to the club. 1st XI Team Captain, Harold Turner, or H as he is affectionately known, rejoined the club six years ago after playing for Hampton 30 years previously as a junior. H has inspired the Club over the last few years to achieve success on the field. He is also the groundsman and can be seen tending the hallowed square on most days during the cricket season.

David Blackford, the present Club Captain, came through the junior academy. His wife Bethan is said to make the best teas in the league. His son Morgan, born at the turn of the year, ought to develop into a great cricketer.

At a time when English cricket appears to be in decline, clubs like Hampton-in-Arden have a responsibility to develop and attract more young players. Perhaps Hampton will nurture a player to the level of English test cricket, or find the next Ian Botham.

A Poster created by the Club in 1999 to attract Junior Players to join the Hampton Lions Junior Cricket Club and displayed in the village.

As the new millennium dawns, the Club faces a new future in the Birmingham and District Premier League. The Club's aims for the new millennium are ambitious. It seeks a long-term future at a ground within Hampton-in-Arden village, and also wishes to canvass support and enthusiasm for the coming years.

HAMPTON HARRIERS NETBALL CLUB

In the summer of 1998 the Hampton Harriers Netball Club was founded by three friends; Julie Ainsworth, Kate Cooke and Sonia Hockaday. They were all keen to play, but had discovered that very few teams operate in the Solihull area. Training was advertised to take place on Monday nights at George Fentham School, and the Club soon gained some enthusiastic team-makers.

The first season in the Coventry Netball League was a very tough one for the Harriers; not only did they lose every match with appalling scores, but also had injuries, fines from the League and the loss of promising members. Despite all that the work continued and Sonia, their coach, strove hard to improve individual skills.

In the summer of 1999 new players were recruited thanks to leafleting and an advert in the local paper. Numbers rose once more. New faces appeared and at the AGM in July – Clare Cook, Jill Hall and Kerry Hall joined the committee.

Winter season (1999/2000) training has been taking place at Stoke Park School, Coventry, with another team. This has produced encouraging results. Half the matches have been won and those lost have been closer and certainly enjoyable. The team is deeply committed, and hopefully will continue to go from strength to strength.

Hampton Harriers Netball Team – back row from left:
Karen Desmond, Clare Cook, Joanne Williams, Kerry Hall, Jill Hall and Lucy Minton.
Front row from left Gail Wyldes, Julie Ainsworth, Liz Cross and Kate Cooke.

THE HAMPTON-IN-ARDEN SPORTS CLUB

Organised sport has been played in Hampton for 140 years, starting with a cricket club and followed in 1902 by both hockey and tennis. In 1964 the club moved to its present location, and built a clubhouse. A football club was started, and in 1974 the clubhouse was extended and two squash courts added. To enable the last phase of development to be financed, the Parish Council granted the Sports Club a 28 year lease on the Parish Recreation Ground. The club has provided sporting facilities for the village, under the terms of that lease, until the present day.

The club is a company limited by guarantee and is controlled by its directors. All the current directors live, or were brought up, in Hampton. The day-to-day running of the club is delegated to the management committee, comprised of officers of the company and representatives of the playing sections. The club was set up with no issued share capital and is financed by members' subscriptions, income on investment, bar income and fund-raising. It is stipulated that there will always be seven directors, all unpaid, of whom the majority shall be residents of the village. The clubhouse facilities comprise a general lounge and bar area with satellite digital television, a tennis lounge overlooking the courts, two squash courts, a kitchen and male and female changing rooms with showers.

The club has been successful over the years, as is demonstrated by the fact that it currently fields sixteen senior teams and nine junior teams across the various sports sections. The teams compete in local, regional and national leagues. Each section runs its own social events, including Quiz Nights, Discos and Annual Dinners. The Sports Club held a very successful Mid-Summer Ball during 1999 in a marquee erected alongside the pavilion.

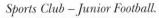

Sports Club – Junior Football.

The Hockey Section

There is a total of 151 senior players in this section, forming eight teams, and 63 junior players, currently being coached and forming two teams. The Ladies' First team achieved the National League Division 2 status towards the end of the 1990s and the men play in the DTZ Premier Division. The National Hockey Association insists that league games are played on synthetic surfaces and so Hampton plays its home games at Bablake School, Coventry and Warwick University.

Over the last ten years the Sports Club has sought planning permission for an Astroturf pitch and floodlights on the Recreation Ground, together with improvements to the clubhouse facilities. This culminated in a public inquiry in 1999 at which planning permission was refused.

The hockey section has produced over 30 players at County level and above. Robert Clift represented England and Great Britain and was a Gold Medal winner at the Seoul Olympics. Sally Watson has also played with the full England squad.

A ladies team from the Hockey section of the Sports Club won the Midland Premier League in 1998.
Front row from left – Karen Juniper, Alison Barber, Becky Weaver, Emma Curtis, Jean Scott Miller,
Marie Laure-Rigg and Lucy Anne Snelson.
Back row from left – Teresa Cannell (Manager), Julie Parry, Julie Haig, Jane Allen, Clare O'Hara, Helen
Gaunt, Nic Gotrel, Sally Watton, Vicky Watts, Sue Sutton (coach), ? (physio) and Sheena Mackintosh.

The Football Section

There are 24 senior members in this section. The senior soccer team plays in the Carnation Premier 1 League. Last season they won this league, the Midlands Sunday Invitation Cup and the Keeley Cup. There are 83 junior members being coached and playing in teams at U/7s and U/14s.

The Tennis Section

The club – at first formed for the use and enjoyment by families in the village – is still well attended. It has 62 senior members and 59 juniors. The club is now represented by one men's and three ladies' teams in the Coventry and District Leagues, and is hoping to increase the men's teams to three during the coming season. The three courts were re-surfaced in 1998/9.

There is a very active junior section of which eighty per cent are children from the village. Regular coaching sessions are held for these juniors throughout the year.

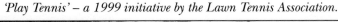

'Play Tennis' – a 1999 initiative by the Lawn Tennis Association.

Tennis – The 1999 Club Championship Awards.

The Squash and Racketball Section

The squash courts were completely refurbished in 1999 following severe flood damage. The section fields two men's and one ladies' squash teams playing in the local leagues, and one racketball team. The annual club tournament is held during April and is well supported.

The Boules Section

The boules piste was laid during the early 1990s. There are now 16 teams playing in two divisions throughout the summer. Each team consists of four players and is organised by groups from the village: the village pubs, clubs and other associations. In 1999 the league was won by a team from the White Lion Inn.

Chapter Six:

Village Events

Anumber of special events take place within the village; some involve a small group of people and some involve most of the village. They vary from special interest topics to events which have a much wider appeal. This section details some of these events but it does not pretend to be an exhaustive list of events – just a selection of the many that take place. Most of these have been selected because they are considered to be special Hampton events. Thus there is no description of the Bonfire night parties although these do take place, notably at the Cricket Club and the Fentham Club. All of the organisations and clubs within the village run events of one sort or another. These are mentioned in the descriptions of those clubs and organisations. Here is a sample of some extra special events which have not been organised by any of the aforementioned village organisations.

MILLENNIUM CELEBRATIONS

Never a community to miss an opportunity for a party, Hampton joined with all of the rest of the world in celebrating the arrival of the year 2000. Judging by the lights, fireworks, marquees and general sounds of merriment, there were dozens of different celebrations going on all over the village. Many parties and huge amounts of fun and games ... but to the hundred or so folk who were there, *the* party was the Millennium Celebration Buffet Dance at Fentham Hall. How many parties has that Hall witnessed? It wasn't there at the end of the first millennium, but has housed enough parties to make it seem like that.

What a great place it is for a village *do*, and the village is lucky to have such a wealth of talent and enthusiasm and cooking skills in the village. The chief organiser of the Fentham Hall Dance has already been publicly thanked, and is too modest to wish that she be named; but as RE herself commented, there really were very many hands making light work in the days before the 'do' and on the morning after. It was a really co-operative effort in the true Hampton tradition.

This was an event with enough glitz to rival The Dome! Music for all tastes and food sufficient almost for the proverbial 5000. The *buffet* turned out to be little short of a banquet (with six varieties of main dish). No detail had been

At the Millennium Eve Party in the Fentham Hall.

spared (even down to a welcoming champagne cocktail), with the beautiful blue and gold and silver decoration of the hall and the table settings: lights, candles, flowers, souvenir wine glasses, menu cards – everything coordinated and not a single detail overlooked.

After the amazing supper there was dancing and partying, with occasional forays outside to that excellent viewing area – the car park (arguably the best view point in Hampton). Viewers could take in the great panorama of lights and fireworks to the south and west.

Soon it was time for the strokes of Big Ben and then *Auld Lang Syne* with memories and reflections that always come with it. And then, more reflection for the many who joined John de Wit in the parish church whose own Millennium will be celebrated in 2130. A moving, candlelit service of hymns and prayer for the new century .... a fitting farewell to the past and a welcome and a blessing for a better world tomorrow.

THE ANNUAL ARTS AND CRAFTS EXHIBITION

The annual Arts & Crafts Exhibition is jointly organised by Hampton Community Crafts and the Hampton Society to provide an opportunity for local artists, craft workers and students from Hampton Community Crafts to submit their work for display and, if they wish, to sell. Submissions from artists and craft workers from outside the community are by invitation.

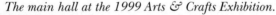

The main hall at the 1999 Arts & Crafts Exhibition.

The exhibition had its beginnings in the late 1970s and has appeared since that time in many guises and at differing venues within the village before settling in the Fentham Hall as a mid-October two-day weekend event. It has now become well established and is an important occasion in the village diary.

The tradition of inviting the Mayor of Solihull formally to open the exhibition provides the only current opportunity for the Mayor to make an official visit to the village, and gets the event off to a splendid start. The high standard of presentation of the exhibits is well supported by flower arrangements produced by students and tutors, adding quality to the general atmosphere.

Another regular feature of the weekend is the attendance of an 'artist/craft worker in residence'. This provides an opportunity within the main exhibition area for the demonstration of special skills: an element of the event that is always appreciated by visitors.

The Children's exhibition on the stage in the main hall at the Arts and Crafts Exhibition.

There is also a display of work produced by children who attended the Summer Art School. Their work is always impressive, amazingly inspirational and extremely diverse in style and content.

A display of photographs presented by the Camera Circle has recently become an established part of the exhibition, showing work produced by conventional means and by digital origination, all to a very high standard.

The event is also a very important shop-window for Hampton Community Crafts. It gives a good opportunity to enrol students in forthcoming classes and workshops. The varying items on display give a fine representation of work that can be produced with guidance from skilled and enthusiastic tutors.

The 1999 resident artist, Lindsay Lloyd, painting on glass in the main hall watched by Shell Hashemi.

THE CHILDREN'S SUMMER ART GROUP

Monet, Picasso and Van Gogh collectors will soon have some new art to admire. Why? Because for two weeks during their summer school holidays lots of Hampton's budding young artists headed for the Scout and Guide Headquarters to do some serious, spectacular, eye-catching art. They are pretty good at craft work too.

These extremely popular classes were run by Katherine Thomas and Lindsay Lloyd, supported by volunteer parents and friends. The classes covered a wide range of ideas and used lots of interesting materials, with the children producing some outstanding work. This year's themes ranged from Space Art to Bowls and Urns to 3D Box Skylines, and much, much more.

Comments from children who attended this year's course include: *"It's very good fun, and I'd definitely do the course again." "I could experiment with materials I'd never used before – it was brilliant." "Every session is different; there is always something new and Art Club can go ahead whatever the weather." "It's fantastic fun every year."*

All the children who took part would like to say a very BIG thank you to Katherine and Lindsay. Everyone is looking forward to future Art Schools, and to displaying their work at the annual Arts and Crafts Exhibition in Fentham Hall in mid-October. So is there a new Van Gogh amongst them? Who knows!

The Children's Summer Art Group in the Scout and Guide Headquarters.

YE OLDE TRIPONIANS ASSOCIATION

A Gastronomical and Musical Evening for Gentlemen.

This unique Hampton event started in 1950 and in the year 2000 celebrated its Gold Anniversary. Little detail is known about its origins, but most believe it began as a gentlemen's evening on the lines of post-war Glee Clubs.

The evening is based around a hearty meal of tripe and onions and, although during recent years it has been refined into tasty sausages and mash with mushy peas, there is still a portion of bleached tripe and onion sauce as a token gesture to the past.

The tongue-in-cheek ceremony is of course entirely meaningless, and the only dress code requirement is a colourful bow tie, which is protected from the hazards of onion sauce by a ceremonial bib.

The singing of a rather dubious anthem is followed by toasts to 'The Queen' and 'The Olde Triponions' past and present, after which everyone takes a cautious sip from an ancient chamber pot known as 'The Loving Cup'.

Held once a year in early March, the evening is the responsibility of a chairman who holds office for just twelve months. His final duty is to choose his successor – an honour which is never refused.

The outgoing chairman becomes the 'Old Mayor' for the following year. Wearing a huge scarlet cloak trimmed with gold and fake fur the Mayor looks most resplendent as he presides over the evening's events.

The 'Tripe Supper' is probably the only Hampton event to appear in the Times newspaper under *Court and Social*, as it did on Friday 10 March 2000.

Ye Olde Triponians Supper.

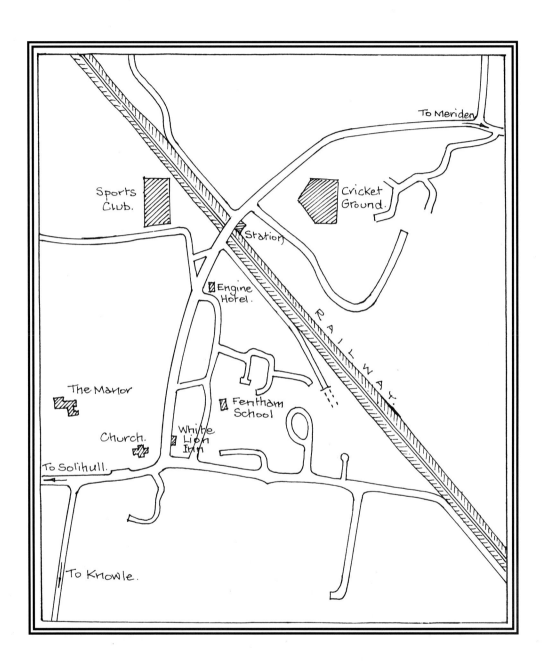

Chapter Seven:

Outside the Village

SURROUNDING THE VILLAGE

The village is generally considered to be the built-up area including all of Old Station Road and, to most people, the houses in Eastcote Lane. This differs from the civil parish of Hampton-in-Arden as Eastcote Lane is in the Parish of Barston and Hampton parish includes the houses in Catherine de Barnes that are to the east of the canal. There are some residents who live outside the area defined above but who regard themselves as Hamptonians.

There are four operational farms in the area as well as several farm houses that are no longer allied to land. In Eastcote Lane, Craddocks Nursery not only grows plants for sale elsewhere but has direct public sales on site. On the right hand side of Meriden Road just at the end of the village is Midfield, a Milbury Care Home catering for up to 8 adults with learning difficulties. Just past Midfield is an old Second World War ammunition dump now known as the Storage Depot. It still retains the storage bunkers for ammunition but the first half of the site is currently being used to store large bags of wood shavings by Arden Wood Shavings based on the Kenilworth Road on the way to Balsall Common. Further on past Patrick Farm on the opposite side of the road is Meriden Mill Farm where a company sells water features for the garden. Both Craddocks and Meriden Mill Farm have resident owners but some businesses such as the craft workshops at Pasture Farm, the offices at Mouldings Green Farm and at Diddington Hall, are occupied only during the day. It seems likely that in the not too distant future there will also be craft workshops in the redundant farm buildings at Patrick Farm.

On the south side of Coventry Road there are a number of businesses including a Solihull M.B.C. waste disposal site. Next to this business is the Jones plant hire business and on the other side is the old Arden Brickworks. On this site bricks were made from local clay and a hole in the ground still exists. This large, and currently water-filled, hole can be seen very near to the footpath that runs off Old Station Road. The site owners S.I.T.A., who also own the Packington landfill site, have planning permission to use this hole and the surrounding land for landfill waste disposal.

HAMPTON LANE FARM

Hampton Lane Farm, land at Church Farm and Hook End Farm, are all farmed as one unit totalling 280 acres. The land is all tenanted and the total rent is approximately £18,000 per annum. The main farm is due west of the village, and the remainder to the south. The soil type is mainly clay, and could be described as very 'loving' when conditions are damp – witness the footpath walkers struggling up the field path from Barston to Hampton on a damp morning!

The land is divided into approximately fifty per cent arable and fifty per cent grass. Mixed farming and rotation might not necessarily be good for profit, but it is good for the land. The arable land is given over to wheat, barley and oilseed rape. Some of the wheat and barley goes for bread and brewing, and some is fed to livestock during the winter. Oil seed rape is sold for crushing, and the oil used in the manufacture of margarine. The amount of land set aside varies from year to year, depending upon the directive from Brussels, and this year it is to be ten per cent of all arable land.

The livestock side of the business consists of 150 beef cattle for fattening. These are grazed during the summer in the small paddocks on the edge of the village. The larger grass fields are used for silage and hay conservation to feed the beef cattle during the winter when they are housed in cattle yards.

The farmer, Tom Moore, and one other man carry out the work on the farm, with help from an outside contractor when necessary. The current returns from wheat and beef do not justify the employment of a man at the moment, but do keep the land and property in reasonable shape.

The current national situation means that life is tough down on the farm. Properties such as this are attractive and productive, deserving to be supported in their endeavours in the new century.

MOULDINGS GREEN FARM

Mouldings Green Farm is owned by Bill Jones who lives in a bungalow on the property with his wife Angela. In order to retain the 83 acres of the farm in a working state he has had to diversify. Four years ago the old redundant farm buildings were converted into offices providing a new source of income.

David Townley, born in Hampton, and still living in the village, has been crucial to the operation of Mouldings Green Farm. He has been the only full-time employee for 32 years. (He received his long-service award at the Royal Agricultural Show after completing 30 years service.)

Mouldings Green Farm is run as a mixed farm: beef, sheep, potatoes, wheat and oil seed rape, plus 14 acres of set-aside.

It has become increasingly difficult to export wheat and oil seed rape owing to present very high exchange rate of the pound necessitating a reduction to 54 acres allocated to the crops.

Mouldings Green Farm – David Townley is presented with his long service award by Lord Iliffe at the Royal Show.

The BSE crisis has been devastating to the beef industry and Bill has had the distressing experience of seeing animals over 30 months of age incinerated, knowing they were perfectly healthy.

All potatoes grown at Mouldings Green Farm are sold at the gate at much lower prices than those of the supermarkets.

Ewe sales prices are now lower than when Bill began farming locally forty years ago, but diversification has allowed him to retain some sheep.

The greater part of farm income at present is from government subsidies received on heads of cattle, sheep and acreage payment on crops, and set-aside. Although current farming is bedevilled by paperwork and is subject to restricting controls, it is still good to see the green fields surrounding Mouldings Green Farm and at the same time receive a regular income through diversification.

OTHER FARMS AROUND HAMPTON

In addition to the above there are two other farms which are considered to be village farms. Home Farm in Shadowbrook Lane is run by Nigel and Keri Redfern. They farm approximately 700 acres which includes land at both Walford Hall

Farm and Diddington Hall Farm. The dairy side of the business is being run down but they still have some store cattle. The farm has about 500 sheep and the arable crops this year include winter wheat, oil seed rape and spring barley. The farm is run with some part time help and the use of contractors for jobs such as silage-making and baling.

Patrick Farm is about 350 acres but two brothers Tom and Adam Beaty run the farm as part of a larger unit of about 1,000 acres. The extra acreage is made up of two parcels of land, one of which, like Patrick Farm is owned by the Packington Estate with another owner for the third parcel of land. The total landholding is split approximately 50/50 between arable and livestock. There are approximately 600 breeding ewes and about 300 cattle in all including 125 suckling cows and their calves, the remainder being store cattle. Arable crops include oil seed rape, wheat, barley and beans. The only additional help on the farm is part-time.

HAMPTON AND THE OUTSIDE WORLD

The high value of properties and the situation of the village in the Green Belt has ensured that many busy and successful people live here. The village school takes a large proportion of children of primary school age, but most secondary school children travel to neighbouring Solihull, Coventry, Birmingham, Balsall Common and other places; school buses are a feature of life in term time.

The residents of many houses in the village travel to and work in neighbouring towns mainly by car or train, and the distances involved are often surprisingly great. Three or four persons are known to travel daily to London, and many others use Hampton as a centre to go to a variety of workplaces all over the country. The last coach of the London Express out of Coventry contains a regular group of daily travellers from Hampton and surrounding areas.

Hampton residents make an impact upon the commercial and professional life of the whole region. Several Hamptonians run their own businesses in Birmingham, Solihull and elsewhere; large firms make considerable use of villagers on their senior staff, whilst the number of academics, accountants, lawyers, doctors, dentists and other professionals is legion. It has been noted that the number of women in this group of professionals has increased in recent years. The convenience of the station and its useful services explain why many commuters live here. They form quite a phalanx on morning and evening trains in and out of Birmingham and Coventry. It is, of course, impossible to quantify their contribution to the working life of the region, but it must be considerable.

Many of the people who have passed their working lives commuting from Hampton choose to retire here, swelling the membership of groups such as Probus and providing a nucleus of people who engage in recreational and educational activities beyond the limits of the village. Many villagers are, for example, members of extra-mural classes of Birmingham and Warwick Universities; others swell the ranks of the University of the Third Age and are patrons of the Arts in the area.

The people of Hampton are great travellers. Speak to any villager and he or she will tell you about distant places. Groups like The Has-Beens go as parties to places like Goa; other friendly groups of neighbours visit interesting sites for walking in the United Kingdom. Most of the cruise liners have seen Hamptonians aboard. And because Birmingham International Airport is a mere three miles away, fly-away holidays are within easy reach. Already a large proportion of villagers can claim to have used the Channel Tunnel by rail or car, and of course new attractions like the Dome are within the experience of some people from the village.

The proximity of the Airport and the NEC also means that visitors from overseas are a common sight here. There are known to be at least a dozen providers of bed and breakfast in the village, and Hamptonians have friends from all over the world who visit from time to time. A few are known to have relatives through marriage from mainland Europe, America and even the Far East. Hampton must be a prime example of a small attractive Green Belt community, quiet and typically English, which is in reality at the centre of a complex of national and international connections. And how many are already on or use the World Wide Web? You can't count them on ten fingers.